Blair,

Thank you for your partnership in sharing the Gospel of Jesus through God's Word and making the impossible possible.

D

THE
Impossible
Dream

The UNSTOPPABLE JOURNEY
of GOD'S WORD BEHIND
the IRON CURTAIN *and* BEYOND

Bob Burckle *and* Dirk Smith

This book is dedicated to all who have risked their lives for the sake of the Gospel—brave men and women who carried the light of truth into the darkest corners of the world.

To those who have gone before us, laying the foundation of faith with their courage, sacrifice, and unwavering trust in God—thank you for paving the way.

And to those who will rise to answer the call, carrying forward the mission of spreading God's Word to every nation—may you be inspired by these stories and empowered by His Spirit.

Table of Contents

Table of Contents v

Letter To The Reader xi

The Story of EEM
Isaiah 6:8. xiii

PIONEERS AND FOUNDATION STORIES

The Impossible Dreamer: Gwen Hensley's Vision
1961 *Acts 20:24* 2

The Traveling Bible: Revival Sparked by a Train Guard
1970s *Isaiah 55:11* 6

Vienna's Role: A Gateway of Grace in the Cold War
1960s *Exodus 15:2* 10

Karolina's Quiet Defiance: Faith in Communist Czechoslovakia
1962 *Joshua 1:9.* 13

Confiscated, Not Silenced: God's Word at a Soviet Border
1960s *Isaiah 40:8* 16

Persecution and Praise: Romania's Awakening
1960s *Matthew 5:10* 20

Faith Through a Child's Eyes: Smuggling Stories of Innocence
1960s - 1980s *Matthew 18:3.* 24

Shadows and Light: The Secret Police Files
1969 *Luke 8:17* 28

Brother D's Defiance: Letters of Light in Hostile Lands
1974 *Romans 8:31*. 31

Bob Hare's Question: Balancing Hunger and Eternity
1980s *Matthew 4:4*. 35

Hidden Faith: When Cardinals Smuggle and Principals Preach
1980s *Matthew 13:44* 39

PERSONAL TRANSFORMATION STORIES

Oleg's Story: Finding Light in Russia's Spiritual Void
1980s *Hosea 4:6*. 44

Victor's Redemption: From Shadows to Shepherd
1990s *Hebrews 8:12* 48

Sacred Whispers: Igor's Journey from Secret Baptism to
Kingdom Builder in Russia
1990s *Psalm 119:49-50* 51

From Soviet Captain to Kingdom Captain:
Igor's Transformation
1990s *1 Corinthians 1:18* 56

Faina's Freedom: From Prison to a Life of Ministry
2000s *John 8:32*. 61

Lida's Awakening: From Asylum to Authentic Faith
2003 *2 Corinthians 5:17* 64

Worth Everything: Elena's Unshakable Faith
2010s *Romans 12:12*. 67

Galena's Leap of Faith: Breaking the Chains of Atheism
2010s *Philippians 2:13*. 72

Masoud's Miracle: From Drowning to Discipleship
2010s *Isaiah 43:2*. 75

Table of Contents

Yasser and Zahra: Love Stronger Than Tradition
    2010s *Galatians 3:28* 78

Reconciled Brothers: A Shia-Sunni Journey to Unity
    2010s *Ephesians 2:14* 81

Prison Walls to Open Hearts: Brother CC8's Mission
    2015 *Hebrews 13:3* 84

Former Foes, United in Christ: Serbian-Croatian Reconciliation
    2010s *Ephesians 4:32* 87

Marina's Awakening: From Confusion to Christ
    2020s *Psalm 119:130* 91

From War to Worship: Constantine and Anastasia's Journey
    2022 *Matthew 11:28.* 94

The Nurse's Return: A Divine Appointment in Lithuania
    2020s *Romans 8:28* 97

Tetyana's Awakening: When Age Finds Truth
    2022 *Isaiah 46:4* 100

BIBLE DISTRIBUTION AND IMPACT

The Bulgarian Revival: How One Bible Sparked a Movement
    2018 *Hebrews 4:12.* 104

The Thessaloniki Encounter: A Bible 12 Years in Waiting
    2010s *Proverbs 16:9* 107

Opening Hearts Through Education: Ukraine's Ministry of
Education Story
    2015 *Proverbs 22:6.* 110

The Power of Partnership: Hellenic Ministries and
the Farsi Bible Project
    2016 *Ephesians 3:20* 114

Breaking Boundaries: Slovenia's Interfaith Bible Mission
2010s *Psalm 133:1* 118

Macedonia's Revival: Building Sacred Bridges
2020s *Ephesians 4:3* 121

Samuel's Mission: A Child's Passion for Sharing God's Word
2021 *1 Timothy 4:12* 124

Bibles in the Digital Age: Mihai and Sebastian's Mission
2020s *Psalm 96:3* 127

The Chocolate Bar Trade: Revival in Romania
2020s *Matthew 5:6* 130

Vadim's Vision: Overcoming Obstacles for Faith
2020s *2 Corinthians 5:7* 133

Eastern Whispers: Alexander's Kazakh Mission
2020s *Romans 10:15* 136

FAITH IN CRISIS AND CONFLICT

A Warehouse of Hope: God's Word in Kyiv's Darkness
2022 *Psalm 119:105* 140

Faith in Belarus: Bibles and Peace Amid Political Unrest
2020 *Matthew 5:9* 145

Crossing Barriers: God's Work in Divided Cyprus
2020s *Galatians 3:28* 148

Sanctuaries in War: Faith in Rivne's Bomb Shelters
2022 *Psalm 46:1* 151

Hope Among Ruins: Ministry in Ukraine's War Zones
2022 *Matthew 25:35* 154

Divine Choreography: Guardians and Exodus in Avdiivka
2023 *Isaiah 43:2* 157

Table of Contents

Klavdiya's Twelve Days: When Angels Feed Goats
2023 *Psalm 23:4* 161

Morning Star's Vigil: The Watchmen of Vinnytsia
2023 *Isaiah 9:2*. 165

Ashes to Hope: Hidden Treasures in Ukraine's Villages
2023 *Psalm 34:18* 168

The Porto Astro Awakening: God's Movement
Among Refugees
2023 *Jeremiah 29:11*. 171

Six Kilometers from War: The Miracle of Siversk
2023 *Isaiah 41:10* 174

Hope in Kramatorsk: When Bombs Build Faith
2023 *2 Corinthians 4:6* 177

REACHING THE MARGINS:
MINISTRY AMONG THE OVERLOOKED

Ana's Love: A Shelter for Croatia's Forgotten Children
2010s *James 1:27*. 182

Toncka's Courage: Love in Forgotten Roma Villages
2010s *1 John 4:18*. 185

Mahdi's Journey: Grace in an Afghan Refugee's Life
2010s *Luke 19:10*. 188

Grace in the Margins: The Hooligans' Church in
the Czech Republic
2020s *Matthew 9:12-13*. 191

Hope Behind Bars: The Women's Prison Ministry
2020s *Luke 4:18* 194

Vladimir's Ministry: Love Beyond Grief
2020s *Psalm 147:3*. 197

A Policeman's Prayer: Faith Born in Crisis
  2020s *Psalm 34:4* 200

Rama's Calling: Transforming Roma Communities with Faith
  2020s *Isaiah 52:7* 203

Simple Acts, Profound Impact: Ministry in Romanian Villages
  2023 *1 John 3:18* 206

Serhiyko's Light: A Child's Faith in the Face of War
  2022 *Matthew 19:14.* 209

INTERGENERATIONAL FAITH

Branko's Legacy: Five Generations of Resilient Faith
  2020s *Psalm 103:17* 214

Lev's Testament: A Child's Faith in Exile
  2022 *Isaiah 11:6* 217

Revival in Samokov: When God Breaks Down Walls
  2023 *Colossians 3:11* 220

Conclusion 223

Letter To The Reader

Dear Reader,

In the quiet corners of prison cells and refugee camps, in bomb shelters and Romani villages, in corporate offices and on bustling city streets, God is weaving stories of redemption that defy human explanation. These pages hold glimpses of those stories—sacred moments captured in words, yet pointing to realities far greater than we can imagine.

As you read, we invite you to look closely. Look for the crises that challenge faith and reveal the brokenness of this world. Look for the reconciliation that only God can bring—restoring what was shattered and making enemies into brothers and sisters. And look for the transformation that changes lives, communities, and even nations. These are the threads that run through every story in this book, and they testify to the unstoppable power of God's Word.

You'll read of Bibles tossed from train windows that multiplied thirty-fold in underground churches. You'll see enemies sitting together at a refugee kitchen, reconciled over shared spaghetti. You'll marvel at children leading entire villages to faith, and technology experts turning lines of code into tools of grace. Every narrative pulses with this undeniable truth: **God's Word cannot be contained, controlled, or confined.**

These stories remind us that God is opening doors we couldn't have imagined in places we wouldn't have dared to dream about. From prison cells to tech-based spaces, He is using the most unlikely people and circumstances to accomplish His purposes. A Cardinal smuggling Bibles during the Cold War. A former Taliban recruit becoming an evangelist. A gambling software developer transforming his skills to share the Gospel online. Over and over, we see how God delights in using the unexpected to bring His Word to life.

But this dream goes far beyond Eastern Europe. It stretches to the ends of the earth. The stories you'll read in this book are just the beginning—signposts of what God has already done and promises of what He is still building. His faithfulness spans generations, crosses borders, and breaks through barriers, and there is so much more to come.

As you read, remember that these stories are more than testimonies—they are invitations. Invitations to witness God's faithfulness, to be encouraged in your own faith, and to join in the incredible work He is doing around the world. Some of these accounts will challenge what you believe is possible. Others will stir your heart with awe and gratitude. All of them will point to the God who still works miracles, who still transforms lives, and who is still sending His Word to the furthest corners of the earth.

You are not just turning pages—you are stepping onto holy ground. In these testimonies of divine pursuit and human response, you'll see God's unstoppable plan to reconcile all things to Himself. May these stories deepen your faith, widen your vision, and inspire you to join in this life-changing mission.

For His Word and His Glory,

Bob Burckle and Dirk Smith
Eastern European Mission

The Story of EEM

"Then I heard the voice of the Lord saying,
'Whom shall I send? And who will go for
us?' And I said, 'Here am I. Send me!'"

ISAIAH 6:8

I N THE GATHERING dusk of 1961, a young couple stood at the rail of a ship bound for Vienna, their hearts full of what many called an impossible dream. Gwen and Gayle Hensley, barely in their mid-twenties, carried little more than faith and a burning vision: to bring God's Word to millions trapped behind the Iron Curtain. They couldn't have known then how their simple act of obedience would spark a revolution of hope that would span continents and generations.

Back in American church buildings, faithful believers dropped coins into coffee cans, each metallic ping a prayer for those who hungered for Scripture in lands where faith itself was forbidden. These humble offerings would become seed money for what God would grow into EEM—a testament to how divine providence delights in using the small to accomplish the magnificent.

From a modest printing facility in Vienna, positioned like a lighthouse at the edge of darkness, Bibles began moving eastward through channels that only God could have designed. The stories from these early years read like pages from the book of Acts—Bibles smuggled page by page through border checkpoints, sacred words hidden in false-bottom suitcases, precious Scripture thrown from train windows only to multiply thirty-fold in underground churches.

These were years of holy ingenuity, when God's people learned to be "wise as serpents and gentle as doves." Christians traveling to Soviet bloc countries would carry "a few" Bibles, each journey a victory of faith over fear. Local partnerships formed across denominational lines, united by a common hunger for God's Word. As demand grew, EEM established its own printing operations in Vienna, transforming what began as a trickle into a river of living water flowing eastward.

When the Soviet Union fell in the early 1990s, doors that had been sealed for generations suddenly swung open. The ministry that had operated in shadows stepped into the light, ready to meet an unprecedented spiritual hunger. Countries that once banned religious literature now welcomed it, and EEM's years of faithful preparation positioned them to respond with wisdom and grace.

Today, that original vision has expanded beyond anything the Hensleys might have imagined. EEM's work spans 36 nations in 32 languages, reaching from the Balkans to Central Asia. The methods have evolved—from smuggled pages to digital Scripture, from hidden Bible studies to partnerships with Orthodox churches—but the mission remains unchanged: we want everyone to have God's Word in their heart language.

Recent years have seen God write new chapters in this ongoing story. In 2020, ancient walls crumbled as the Macedonian Orthodox Church partnered with EEM to place children's Bibles in young hands across their nation. When war erupted in Ukraine in 2022, EEM's network became a lifeline of hope, delivering both bread for the body and food for the soul to those in crisis.

Yet perhaps the most profound testament to God's faithfulness lies not in the millions of Bibles distributed or the borders crossed, but in the individual lives transformed. In prison cells where chains fall away, in refugee kitchens where ancient hatreds dissolve, in Roma villages where children lead their parents to faith—here we witness the living power of God's Word to penetrate the deepest darkness.

The story of EEM reminds us that God's Word will not return void. Whether carried in diplomatic pouches or hidden in lines of code, whether read in palace chambers or bomb shelters, Scripture continues to accomplish all that He purposes. From those first prayers on a Vienna-bound ship to today's digital distribution networks, each chapter reveals the extraordinary lengths to which God will go to reach those who seek Him.

This is more than an organizational history—it's a testament to divine faithfulness, human courage, and the unstoppable power of God's Word to find those who hunger for truth. As we look toward the future, we stand in awe of how God continues to use ordinary people to accomplish extraordinary things, one page, one life, one miracle at a time.

Pioneers and Foundation Stories

The Impossible Dreamer:

Gwen Hensley's Vision

1961

---

*"However, I consider my life worth nothing to
me; my only aim is to finish the race and complete
the task the Lord Jesus has given me—the task
of testifying to the good news of God's grace."*

ACTS 20:24

I N 1961, AS autumn leaves danced across Oklahoma soil,
a young couple stood at a crossroads that would alter the
spiritual landscape of Eastern Europe forever. Gwen Hensley,
barely twenty-four years old, and his wife Gayle gazed toward

a horizon that stretched far beyond their small-town roots. In their hearts burned what many dismissed as an impossible dream: bringing God's Word to millions trapped behind the Iron Curtain.

The scene that catalyzed their commitment unfolded in a Romanian village several years later, where Gwen encountered a reality that would haunt and inspire him for the rest of his life. The entire village shared a single Bible—some portions of it carefully preserved in handwritten fragments on precious scraps of paper. Standing there, watching weathered hands pass these sacred copies among the faithful, tears streamed down his face. Turning to Gayle, he spoke words that would echo through decades: "If it is the Lord's will, and I believe it is, I am going to see that these people get the Bible in their language."

Born in Victory, Oklahoma in 1937, Gwen carried the irony of his birthplace's name into a mission field where victory seemed impossible. Yet from those humble beginnings, God would forge a man whose influence would reach from peasant villages to royal courts. He moved easily between worlds—equally comfortable with diplomats and farmers, Austrian nobility and village pastors. But his heart belonged to those who hungered for God's Word, and his days were consumed with finding innovative ways to satisfy that hunger.

"We went forth in 1961 on a quest," he wrote to Gayle in 1984, "a quest that was laughed at by our friends and families. It was an impossible dream. We were seen as ragtag children, chasing windmills on the frontier of civilization." Yet through their faithful persistence, what seemed like quixotic tilting at windmills became a revolution of hope that would outlive its dreamer.

When cancer claimed Gwen in 1985 at just forty-seven years old, many wondered if the dream would survive its dreamer. But God had other plans. The small operation that began with coffee can collections in American Bible classes had grown into a sophisticated ministry serving millions. The vision that once seemed impossible outgrew Gwen's vision and was carried forward by those who caught glimpses of God's heart through Gwen's eyes.

In his final letter to Gayle, written just months before his death, Gwen's words captured the essence of a life poured out for others: "I just want to right the unrightable wrong -- to love people who owed me nothing and who would not finger me out in a crowd if I had not gone. But I loved them from afar because I had been loved by God and forgiven of my sins."

An Impossible Dream
(EXCERPTS FROM LETTERS TO GAYLE
FROM GWEN HENSLEY, MARCH 1964)

I am a Christian, a son of God. I live for the day to be taken home to live for and with Him. However, I am human and the father of our child and your husband. I think God can understand my feeling on the subject and therefore will forgive my desire to stay on earth with you.

We went forth in 1961 on a quest–a quest that was laughed at by our friends and families. It was an impossible dream. We were seen as ragtag children, chasing windmills in the forest of civilization.

- *We went out to fight the "unbeatable foe" — only he was beatable because God was on our side.*
- *We went out to bear "unbearable sorrow" — only it was bearable because God was with us.*
- *To run where the brave dare not go, because in our youth and inexperience we didn't know what to be afraid of because of our confidence in the Lord.*
- *I just want to right the unrightable wrong—to love—to love people who owed me nothing and who would not finger me out in a crowd if I had not gone. But I loved them from afar because I had been loved by God and forgiven of my sins.*

At this point in time despite a new intrusion into my body and spirit, this is still my quest to follow that star. To fight for right without question or pause—to be willing to march into hell for a heavenly cause.

I shall seek this quest till I am laid to rest. The quest of trying to grasp the lost in Eastern Europe. I know that without faith and God's love and grace they will be lost but I know that if I am knowing of one to this quest. I can rest for all eternity. The rest of the song you know.

Questions for Reflection:
- What "impossible dreams" has God placed in your heart?
- How do you respond when others call your vision foolish?
- What legacy of faith are you building for future generations?
- Where might God be calling you to "right the unrightable wrong"?

Points for Prayer:
- For the continuing impact of seeds planted by early visionaries
- For courage to pursue God-given dreams despite obstacles
- For wisdom in carrying forward the legacy of faith
- For those still waiting to receive their first Bible
- For new dreamers to arise with vision for Bible distribution

Prayer Response:
Lord of impossible dreams, we thank You for visionaries like Gwen who dared to believe You for the seemingly impossible. His legacy reminds us that no vision is too bold when it aligns with Your purposes. Thank You for the countless lives transformed because one young couple said "yes" to Your call. Give us courage to dream big dreams for Your Kingdom, knowing that You are able to do exceedingly abundantly above all we ask or imagine. Help us live lives that inspire future generations to trust You for the impossible.

The Traveling Bible:

Revival Sparked by a Train Guard

1970s

*"So is my word that goes out from my mouth:
It will not return to me empty."*

ISAIAH 55:11

THE TRAIN RATTLED through Eastern Europe's misty landscape, its wheels clicking a steady rhythm against cold steel rails as it traced the edge of the Iron Curtain. Inside one of the worn compartments, Ivan Martos, an employee of the National Bank of Hungary, held his briefcase closer as uniformed guards moved methodically through the car. His heart wasn't racing because of irregular documents—everything about his official position was meticulously in order. No, the thunder in his chest came from what lay hidden within that leather case: a Bible that was about to embark on an extraordinary journey of its own.

A uniformed guard asked Mr. Martos for his travel papers and then to open his briefcase. The guard's loud, angry voice cut like a blade through the train's steady rumble. "What is a man in your position doing with a Bible?" Before Ivan could form a response, the sacred book was already sailing through the open window of the moving train, now just a dark silhouette against the gathering dusk. In that moment of apparent defeat, no one could have guessed how God would transform this act of hostility into a miracle of multiplication.

Two years passed, each day adding weight to the seeming loss. Then, on another train journey to Vienna, Ivan could barely contain his joy as he bounded into the EEM office, his face glowing with the kind of radiance that only comes from witnessing divine providence. "I got my Bible back!"

The story he shared left his listeners speechless, their coffee growing cold as they leaned forward to catch every word. A package had arrived at his home days before, containing his weathered but intact Bible. But it was the accompanying note that revealed God's extraordinary handiwork:

"Some of our children were playing along the railroad tracks when they discovered your Bible," the letter began. "Word spread quickly through our village. Several of our older residents remembered owning Bibles before they were banned, and they recalled the power and significance of God's Word." What happened next was completely unplanned—it was as if God Himself orchestrated it.

"We made a collective decision to keep the discovery secret while those who felt drawn to its message made handwritten copies. This labor of love lasted two years. We hope you can forgive us for keeping your Bible for so long. But we thought you might find joy in knowing that we are now a secret fellowship of thirty believers who have baptized each other and seek to follow Jesus in our daily lives."

What the guard had intended as an act of destruction, God had transformed into an instrument of multiplication. One Bible, cast aside in anger, had become the seed of an entire congregation. Through water-stained pages and handwritten copies, thirty souls had discovered the living Christ. Each carefully transcribed word became a testament to their hunger for truth, proving that even when Scripture is cast aside, it never returns void.

The story spread through underground churches like a flame catching dry tinder, igniting hope in hearts that had grown cold under decades of religious oppression. It reminded believers of how God's Word had survived centuries of attempts to destroy it–from ancient book burnings to modern prohibitions. Even now, in the shadows of Communist control, that same Word was sprouting new life from the very soil where it had been cast.

Years later, when asked about the incident, Ivan would often touch his Bible's worn cover with reverence before speaking. "We forget sometimes," he would say, "that God's Word is living and active. It's not just ink on paper–it's a seed that grows wherever it lands. Even when it's thrown away, it finds fertile soil. Even when it's rejected, it returns with a harvest."

This extraordinary multiplication from a single Bible became a powerful reminder that God's Word can never be truly lost or destroyed. Like the bread and fish that fed thousands from a small boy's lunch, or the mustard seed that grows into a mighty tree, one Bible cast from a train window had become spiritual food for thirty hungry souls. Their story stands as a testament to the unstoppable power of Scripture to find its way into hearts prepared by divine providence, even in the most unlikely circumstances.

Questions for Personal Reflection:

- How has God used apparent setbacks in your life to advance His kingdom?
- When have you seen God multiply His Word in unexpected ways?
- What "lost" opportunities in your life might God be preparing to redeem?

Points for Prayer:

- For those secretly copying and sharing Scripture in restricted nations
- For protection of underground believers and their precious copies of God's Word
- For multiplication of Scripture in creative ways
- For courage for those facing persecution for possessing God's Word
- For those still waiting to receive their first Bible

Prayer Response:

Lord of lost and found, we marvel at Your ability to use even acts of destruction for Your glory. Thank You that no copy of Your Word is ever truly lost. Help us trust that even when we can't see the results, You are working through Your Word in ways we cannot imagine. Give us courage to carry Your truth wherever You send us, knowing that You watch over Your Word to perform it.

Vienna's Role:

A Gateway of Grace in the Cold War

1960s

(WITH CONTRIBUTION FROM SCOTT HAYES,
PUBLISHING DIRECTOR FOR EEM)

*"The Lord is my strength and my defense;
he has become my salvation."*

EXODUS 15:2

I N THE SHADOW of the Iron Curtain, where East met West
in a delicate dance of diplomacy and danger, God was orchestrating a divine strategy that would transform a city of spies

into a fountain of living water. Vienna, positioned by divine providence at the crossroads of competing ideologies, would become not just a hub of Cold War intrigue, but a gateway through which God's Word would flow to spiritually parched nations.

The story begins in the early 1960s, when seven American couples—bright-eyed twenty-somethings with hearts aflame for mission—arrived in Vienna with what seemed like a modest missionary vision. Yet God, the master strategist, had positioned these youthful servants there for purposes far beyond their initial understanding. When Soviet tanks crushed the Prague Spring of 1968, these missionaries discovered their first divine appointment–their church buildings and offices becoming sanctuaries for Czech refugees fleeing oppression.

What started as an emergency shelter soon evolved into something more profound. The simple act of producing Bible pamphlets in Czech language grew into a broader vision that would eventually culminate in the construction of a modern printing facility in 1979–a testimony to how God often grows mighty oaks from the smallest seeds of obedience.

The facility itself became a parable of God's multifaceted purposes. Housing both a printing press for Bible production and a local German-speaking church, it demonstrated how the same space could serve both as a source of written truth and a community of living truth.

Vienna's unique position as a neutral city made it both a diplomatic meeting point and a center of espionage. While intelligence agencies from East and West wove their webs of secrets, God's people engaged in their own covert operations–smuggling Bibles instead of state secrets, trafficking in eternal truth rather than temporal intelligence. The city buzzed with spies serving earthly Kingdoms, while quiet servants of a higher Kingdom moved precious cargo across heavily guarded borders.

The constant flow of refugees through Vienna created an

unprecedented opportunity for ministry. Each wave of displaced souls—Czechs, Hungarians, and others fleeing communist regimes—found not just physical refuge but spiritual sustenance through the Bibles and Christian literature provided in their heart languages. In God's divine orchestration, even forced displacement became a channel for spiritual awakening.

Questions for Reflection:

- How does God use geopolitical circumstances for His divine purposes?
- Where do we see similar "gateway cities" today that God might be positioning for His purposes?
- What role does strategic positioning play in God's Kingdom work?

Points for Prayer:

- For wisdom to recognize divine positioning in our own lives
- For cities currently serving as gateways for God's Word
- For those engaged in Bible distribution in restricted areas
- For refugees to encounter God's Word in their displacement
- For courage to participate in God's strategic purposes

Prayer Response:

Master Strategist, we marvel at how You positioned Vienna as a gateway for your Word during the Cold War years. Thank You for showing us how You can use neutral spaces for sacred purposes, and how You transform cities of secrets into fountains of truth. Help us recognize similar divine positioning in our own time and place. Give us courage to participate in Your purposes, whether through obvious ministry or covert service. May we, like those faithful servants in Vienna, play our part in Your greater strategy of reaching hungry souls with Your truth.

Karolina's Quiet Defiance:

Faith in Communist Czechoslovakia

1962

> *"Be strong and courageous. Do not be afraid;*
> *do not be discouraged, for the Lord your God*
> *will be with you wherever you go."*

JOSHUA 1:9

I N THE SHADOWED landscape of 1962 Czechoslovakia, where official churches operated under strict state regulations and unofficial gatherings risked severe consequences, God was writing a story of courage through a woman named Karolina. Her tale begins not in grand cathedrals but in the quiet corners of

Communist control, where faith often bloomed most beautifully in hidden spaces.

Gwen Hensley first encountered Karolina during a church meeting at a General Assembly gathering–one of the few officially sanctioned religious events in Czechoslovakia. The bonds of faith transcended the artificial boundaries of state control, leading to a deep connection that would reveal the power of persistent faith under pressure.

For years, Karolina carried a deep heartache—her mother lived in Vienna, Austria, beyond the Iron Curtain, while Karolina remained trapped within Czechoslovakia's borders. The Communist authorities repeatedly denied her requests to visit her mother, wielding family separation as a tool of control. Only after her mother's death did they finally grant Karolina permission to travel to Vienna—a bittersweet journey of both grief and her first taste of freedom beyond Communist rule. Yet God's ways are mysterious, and even in the soil of mourning, new seeds of purpose were planted. Upon returning home to Czechoslovakia, Karolina transformed her sorrow into sacred calling, beginning a Bible study in her living room that would eventually lead several souls to baptism, their spiritual rebirth emerging from the very path that began with her grief.

Back in her daily life under Communist rule, Karolina faced perhaps her greatest challenge–living with a Communist son-in-law who viewed her faith with hostility. Yet in this crucible of opposition, she discovered an unexpected ministry: teaching her grandchildren to pray. Even when her son-in-law raged against these quiet lessons of faith, she persisted in planting seeds of truth in young hearts, understanding that God's Word never returns void.

As people began to seek her out for spiritual guidance, Karolina's impact multiplied beyond her family circle. The Word that had sustained her through years of restriction now flowed through her to strengthen others. She became a living testament to how God's truth flourishes even in the most restrictive environments.

Four years before her death, she had become such an inspiration that people traveled long distances just to study the Bible with her. Her life demonstrated a profound truth—that one faithful person, armed with God's Word and unwavering courage, could impact generations. Though she passed away, her memory lived on in the hearts of those who remembered her courage and firm belief in God.

Questions for Reflection:

- How does personal tragedy sometimes open doors for ministry?
- What role does quiet faithfulness play in impacting future generations?
- Where might God be calling us to persist despite opposition?

Points for Prayer:

- For believers facing family opposition to their faith
- For grandparents seeking to pass on spiritual heritage
- For those ministering in restricted nations
- For wisdom in using times of mourning for God's purposes
- For courage to persist in faith despite persecution

Prayer Response:

Father of the faithful, we thank You for testimonies like Karolina's that remind us how Your truth flourishes even in hostile soil. Thank You for those who quietly persist in sharing faith despite opposition, for grandparents who plant seeds of truth in young hearts, and for every believer who chooses faithfulness over safety. Help us recognize how You can use even our seasons of loss for Your purposes. May we, like Karolina, leave a legacy of unwavering faith that inspires generations to come.

Confiscated, Not Silenced:

God's Word at a Soviet Border

▬

1960s

▬

*"The grass withers and the flowers fall, but
the word of our God endures forever."*

ISAIAH 40:8

I N THE TENSE space of a Soviet border crossing, where cold
bureaucracy met burning faith, God was orchestrating a moment
that would reveal the true power of His Word through its very
opposition. As Gwen and five young men approached the USSR
checkpoint in their car, they were met with the familiar, chilling question that defined an era: "Do you have any guns or Bibles?" That these

two items were equated in the minds of border guards spoke volumes about the perceived power of God's Word in Communist territories.

The scene unfolded like a carefully choreographed drama. Most border guards gave their vehicle the customary cursory inspection, but one official, moved by some divine appointment, meticulously examined every scrap of paper in the glove compartment. There, nestled among German papers, he discovered a single Russian biblical pamphlet–a seemingly insignificant find that would trigger an extraordinary response.

In the cold shadow of the border checkpoint, what had been concealed in love was now exposed in fear. "It was as if we had 100 pounds of heroin or opium," Gwen would later write, noting the painful irony in Lenin's own declaration that "Religion is the opium of the people." The guards' eyes narrowed with suspicion as they ordered the travelers from their vehicle, their hands moving methodically across the fabric of jackets and the folds of pockets—places where hope had been tucked away in faith. Each Bible and tract, carried close to the heart like treasures, was now being pulled into the harsh light of Soviet scrutiny. The travelers stood in silent prayer as their offerings—125 pieces of Christian literature, including twenty-six New Testaments—were gathered before them, each one representing a soul that might have encountered the living Word. What they had carried in their blazers and pockets as seeds of transformation now lay exposed, vulnerable testimonies to a truth that transcended borders and ideologies. In this moment of seeming defeat, they would soon witness how God's purposes find pathways even through the narrowest openings of human resistance.

The six hours that followed became a masterclass in divine perspective. As they were photographed like criminals, interrogated in private rooms, and subjected to the psychological pressure of the "waiting game," these servants of God witnessed firsthand how earthly powers inadvertently validate heaven's authority. Every threat to confiscate their car only served to underscore the trans-formative potential contained in those printed pages.

"The USSR recognizes the power of one printed Bible," Gwen observed, "even if it is separated from any religious teacher." At international borders elsewhere, guards concerned themselves with cigarettes and liquor–temporal commodities of fleeting value. But here, where atheism reigned as official doctrine, twenty-six cop-ies of God's Word provoked a response that testified to its eternal significance.

In the end, the officials made a profound decision that revealed God's hand moving in mysterious ways—while they confiscated all 125 pieces of religious literature, they not only allowed the travel-ers to keep their personal Bibles but permitted them to continue their journey into the country rather than turning them away at the border. This sovereign provision illuminated a powerful truth: "The USSR recognizes the power of one printed Bible even if it is separated from any religious teacher." Even as darkness seemed to prevail, the Light found pathways forward. The authorities, perhaps unknowingly participating in divine purposes, created an opening where seeds of faith could still be planted. Each traveler crossing that threshold with Scripture in hand became a living testimony to how God's Word transcends human barriers—the very border designed to keep truth out became the doorway through which it entered. In this moment of unexpected grace, we glimpse how the Kingdom advances not through force but through faithful presence, how seemingly small permissions can become the fertile soil where transformation takes root..

As they continued their journey, now without their precious cargo meant for hungry souls, Gwen reflected on what seemed a setback but was in fact a revelation: "Just to see how they reacted on the border when they learned we had Bibles was worth the trip, in that you see their estimate of the worth of the Bible and what it can do." In their very opposition, the guards had testified to Scripture's power more eloquently than any sermon could have done.

Questions for Reflection:

- How does opposition to God's Word often reveal its true power?
- Where do we see divine purpose even in apparent setbacks?
- What can we learn from those who fear Scripture's influence?

Points for Prayer:

- For those currently smuggling Bibles into restricted nations
- For wisdom in facing opposition to God's Word
- For authorities who encounter Scripture through confiscation
- For creative ways to share truth despite restrictions
- For courage in the face of intimidation

Prayer Response:

Sovereign Lord, we marvel at how You reveal truth even through attempts to suppress it. Thank You for showing us through experiences like Gwen's that opposition to Your Word often becomes its most powerful testimony. Give courage to those who still carry Scripture across hostile borders, wisdom to those facing interrogation for their faith, and hope to all who hunger for truth in restricted lands. Help us recognize, like those border guards, the true worth of Your Word–not to fear it, but to embrace its transforming power.

Persecution and Praise:

Romania's Awakening

▬

1960s

▬

"Blessed are those who are persecuted
because of righteousness, for theirs
is the Kingdom of heaven."

MATTHEW 5:10

IN THE REMOTE village of Ponelle de sub Munte, Romania,
where faith whispered its defiance in hidden gatherings, God
was orchestrating a divine appointment disguised as disruption.
Gwen Hensley and his companion Brother M had embarked on their
journey carrying a precious cargo–sixty-four Bibles and hundreds

of tracts, each one representing potential spiritual transformation in a land where Scripture was scarce and cherished.

The weathered building they approached held one hundred and eighty souls pressed together in worship, their devotion unadorned by the usual trappings of religious ceremony. No printed hymnals guided their praise—just a few worn papers with handwritten songs, their creases telling stories of shared use and precious worth. Some clutched fragments of Scripture, while only a blessed few possessed complete Bibles. In this gathering that would stretch five hours until afternoon's light faded, faith found its purest expression in spiritual poverty.

The assembly's keen eyes spotted Gwen and Brother M immediately—their clothing marking them as outsiders in a place where even fabric told stories of local craft. Yet what might have been cause for suspicion became an open door as leaders slipped outside, their cautious inquiry turning to welcome when simple Russian biblical pamphlets became letters of introduction.

Miraculous timing revealed itself as Brother M began to speak. Barely twenty minutes into his message, a summons to the police station arrived. But in those precious moments before their departure, a young believer from the congregation quietly gathered forty of their Russian New Testaments and ensured they reached eager hands in the assembly, planting seeds that would grow long after the visitors departed.

At the police station, accusations mounted like gathering storm clouds: being in a restricted area without permission, failing to register with authorities, the alleged crime of distributing religious literature in a communist country. When officials searched their car, they discovered the remainder of their precious cargo—twenty-four Bibles and three hundred tracts, all of which were confiscated and meticulously inventoried on an official document, each item representing a potential connection between hungry souls and divine truth.

Hours stretched into a test of endurance as various officials arrived for consultations. When asked to sign a document listing charges laid against them, they requested time to contact the American Embassy in Bucharest–a divine pause that would prove pivotal. Thirty hours passed without food before they finally received something to eat, their physical hunger a mere shadow of the spiritual hunger they had witnessed in Romanian believers.

What began as harsh interrogation transformed, through heaven's intervention, a critical phone call mentioning three words: "telephone... American... Embassy." Divine sovereignty moved through diplomatic channels, turning threat into unexpected hospitality as hotel arrangements replaced the threat of detention.

Though they surrendered twenty-four Bibles and three hundred tracts to authorities, Gwen's heart overflowed with gratitude knowing that forty Bibles had already found their way into hungry hands before their detention. In God's divine economy, what appeared as loss on an official ledger had already become spiritual gain in the Kingdom's accounting. The seed of God's Word, planted in fertile hearts, would continue to multiply long after this encounter, bearing fruit that official opposition could never contain.

As Gwen would later reflect, tears welling in his eyes, "In the West we cannot appreciate the value of one copy of God's Word... these people can, and I am learning to more every day." This experience reinforced the vision that would drive EEM forward–the conviction that every person deserves access to Scripture in their heart language, regardless of political boundaries or personal cost.

The lost Bibles represented a temporary setback, but the forty that reached their destination would become multiplied testimonies of transformation. Each one would be shared among families, read aloud in secret gatherings, cherished as treasures beyond price. What seemed like defeat in the moment was already becoming victory in the spiritual realm. God's Word never returns void, even when its messengers face temporary detention.

Questions for Reflection:
- How do we respond when divine appointments come disguised as interruptions?
- Where might God be using official opposition to advance His purposes?
- What value do we place on the Scripture we so freely possess?

Points for Prayer:
- For believers gathering in restricted circumstances
- For wisdom in using brief windows of opportunity
- For protection over those distributing God's Word
- For hearts to value Scripture as precious treasure
- For divine intervention in moments of opposition

Prayer Response:
Sovereign Lord, we marvel at how You weave eternal purposes through temporal interruptions. Thank You for showing us through experiences like these how opposition often becomes opportunity in Your hands. Give wisdom to those navigating restrictions on Your Word, courage to those facing interrogation for their faith, and grateful hearts to those of us who freely possess what others count as treasure. May we, like these Romanian believers, learn to value Your Word as worth any price.

Faith Through a
Child's Eyes:

Smuggling Stories of Innocence

───

1960s-1980s

───

"Unless you change and become like little children,
you will never enter the Kingdom of heaven."

MATTHEW 18:3

Heidee's Watch: A Daughter's Testament

IN THE GENTLE shadows of childhood memory, where faith and family intertwined like morning mist through Vienna's hills, God was writing His story through the innocent eyes of a little girl. Heidee Gwen Hensley Whitaker's and sister Hollye Hensley Conway's early years became a living testament to how divine purposes often unfold through the simple trust of children's hearts.

For Heidee, her childhood lullabies came accompanied by the quiet rustle of Bibles hidden beneath mattresses, her dreams guarded by angels as the family car carried its precious cargo across hostile borders. Through a child's eyes, these midnight journeys became sacred adventures—each border crossing a story of God's protection, each hidden Bible a treasure more precious than gold.

The weight of their mission revealed itself through her father's stories—tales of brave souls who risked imprisonment to shelter God's Word, of families searching endless days for loved ones lost to prison cells for the crime of sharing Scripture. Yet even these sobering realities served to deepen rather than diminish her under-standing of faith's true cost.

The Berlin Wall's fall in November 1989 found her a newlywed of three months, her tears of joy streaming down as she watched history unfold on television. "GOD, You did this!" her heart cried out, even as it whispered, "I wish dad was with me to celebrate this!" In that moment of triumph, where concrete crumbled and iron curtains rusted away, she glimpsed the culmination of countless prayers and sacrifices that had marked her childhood years.

Greg's Vista: A Son's Perspective

From the heights of Vienna Woods, where ancient church spires pierced clouds heavy with history, young Greg Hensley gained a different vantage point on God's mysterious ways. Standing beside his father at twilight, gazing toward the dim lights of Bratislava reflecting off distant clouds, he learned how physical proximity often masked spiritual chasms.

Those evening moments became parables of divine purpose, as his father explained how that nearby city–so close they could see its glow–lived in a reality far removed from their own. Beyond those lights, people faced imprisonment for possessing the very Book that sat freely on Greg's bedside table. Through these twilight lessons, Greg learned how privilege carries responsibility, how freedom bears obligation to remember those still bound.

The family car became more than transportation–it transformed into a classroom of sacred subterfuge. That small mattress laid in the back, ostensibly for children's comfort on long journeys, concealed heaven's contraband beneath its innocent appearance. Greg learned how border guards, unwilling to disturb sleeping children, became unwitting participants in God's distribution network.

Together, these siblings' memories paint a portrait of how God writes His story through generations, using even the youngest hearts to carry His truth across man-made barriers. Their childhood games played out against a backdrop of eternal significance, their family vacations doubled as divine missions, and their bedtime stories carried weight far beyond fairy tales.

Questions for Reflection:

- How does God use family life to advance His Kingdom purposes?
- What role can children play in God's work of transformation?
- In what ways can childhood experiences of faith shape adult understanding?

Points for Prayer:

- For families currently serving in restricted access nations
- For children growing up amid ministry challenges
- For wisdom in balancing family life with Kingdom work

- For protection over those using creative means to share truth
- For the next generation to carry forward the torch of faith

Prayer Response:

Father of all generations, we thank You for writing Your story through family lines, using even children's innocent presence to advance Your purposes. Thank You for parents who model costly discipleship, for children who learn faith through living example, and for Your protection over families serving Your Kingdom. Help us recognize how every aspect of family life can become sacred space for Your work. May we, like these faithful families, find ways to weave Your purposes through our daily routines.

Shadows and Light:

The Secret Police Files

1969

---

*"For nothing is hidden that will not
become evident, nor anything secret that
will not be known and come to light."*

LUKE 8:17

I N THE HUSHED depths of Czech archives, where history's
dust mingles with forgotten prayers, God was orchestrating
a revelation that would turn persecution into preservation.
Among countless files documenting Communist oppression lay
an unexpected treasure—surveillance records that would testify

not to the regime's power, but to faith's quiet persistence in the face of opposition.

The year was 1969. While the world watched men leave footprints on the moon, Communist authorities kept their meticulous gaze fixed on a different kind of pioneer. On October 28, they began tracking a young missionary they dubbed "Oklahoma"--Gwen Hensley, whose passion for spreading God's Word had caught the attention of those who sought to suppress it.

Each surveillance report reads like an unintentional gospel narrative. With cold precision, state security agents documented meetings that were actually prayer gatherings, recorded movements that were Bible deliveries, and noted contacts that formed a web of underground believers. In their effort to monitor subversion, they were unknowingly chronicling revival.

Decades later when the Regional Director for Central Eastern Europe discovered these files, the divine irony became clear. Every photograph meant to incriminate instead captured moments of courage. Every detailed report meant to build a case against faith became evidence of its unstoppable advance. What the authorities intended as documentation of criminal activity had become a testament to spiritual dedication.

These yellowed pages whisper a profound truth across the decades: no human opposition can ultimately thwart God's purposes. In His divine narrative, even the machinery of persecution becomes a tool for preservation. The very system designed to stamp out faith instead created a detailed record of its endurance.

Today, as we hold these files that once held such power to intimidate, we witness God's ability to transform every tool of opposition into an instrument of testimony. The code name "Oklahoma" no longer carries the weight of surveillance but stands as a reminder that God's light penetrates even the darkest corners of human resistance.

Questions for Reflection:

- How does knowing your actions for God might be documented by others affect your faith journey?
- When have you seen opposition to God's work actually serve to advance it?
- What legacy of faithfulness are you creating that future generations might discover?

Points for Prayer:

- For believers currently under surveillance for their faith
- For wisdom in documenting God's work for future generations
- For courage to remain faithful despite opposition
- For those currently maintaining secret records about believers
- For the preservation and discovery of testimonies of God's faithfulness

Prayer Response:

Lord of history, we thank You for preserving evidence of Your faithful work through unexpected means. Thank You for the reminder that even surveillance meant for harm can become testimony for Your glory. Give us courage to remain faithful in our mission, knowing that You see and record every act of obedience in Your book of remembrance. Help us to be more concerned with Your approval than man's opposition. May our lives write stories of faithfulness that will encourage future generations, whether through official documents or hidden testimonies.

Brother D's Defiance:

Letters of Light in Hostile Lands

━━━

1974

━━━

"If God is for us, who can be against us?"

ROMANS 8:31

I N THE MIST-SHROUDED corners of Yugoslavia, where morning light filtered through iron bars of communist control, God was writing a story of defiant hope through the most ordinary of instruments—a postman's hands. Here, in the quiet persistence of carefully wrapped packages and precisely penned addresses, heaven's truth found its courier in a man known simply as Brother D.

His ministry unfolded not in the dramatic gestures of public proclamation, but in the sacred minutiae of daily devotion. Each Bible wrapped became a prayer, each address written a declaration of faith, each journey on his motorcycle a pilgrimage of purpose. On some days, he would vary his route, boarding trains with precious cargo, his ordinary presence masking extraordinary purpose. In these seemingly mundane moments, God's eternal purposes found their earthly pathways through the most unexpected channels.

Dawn broke cold and harsh on that January morning in 1974, when truth's cost revealed itself in heavy footfalls and commanding voices. As police officers invaded their sanctuary of service, Brother D. and his wife found themselves confined to chairs—unwilling audience to the ransacking of their home. Through long hours they watched as authorities tore through attic beams and barn rafters, searching for what they deemed contraband but heaven called hope—Bibles and precious lists that represented lifelines to believers across Eastern Europe.

The trial and imprisonment that followed might have crushed a weaker spirit. Yet in the confines of his cell, Brother D's conviction burned brighter, refined rather than diminished by pressure. When legal intervention secured his release, he faced the crossroads that defines every servant's journey—the choice between safety and sacrifice. Under threat of a two-year prison sentence, he chose not retreat but resolve, demonstrating how pressure often becomes the crucible where God's servants discover their most creative expressions of faithfulness.

In the larger city where he relocated, divine providence had already prepared soft soil for truth's seeds. Among his new neighbors were postal workers from conservative religious groups, their own hearts harboring hunger for spiritual authenticity. These unlikely allies—heaven's secret agents in official positions—became essential partners in a renewed mission. Where Brother D once operated alone, God had now provided a network of willing hands.

The postal workers, familiar with the system's inner workings, provided invaluable guidance on avoiding detection. Together, they developed a sophisticated distribution network that surpassed Brother D's former solitary efforts. What began as casual conversations over shared meals evolved into strategic partnerships, with these new friends using their official positions to ensure Bible packages navigated the postal labyrinth undetected. When suspicious officials questioned unusual package patterns, these postal workers would redirect attention, creating safe corridors for God's Word to travel through.

This heavenly arrangement transformed Brother D's setback into spiritual advancement–his ministry didn't merely continue; it expanded. The very pressure designed to extinguish his work instead scattered its embers, igniting new fires of faith throughout the region. Through these heaven-appointed connections, distribution channels multiplied, reaching believers who had previously remained outside his network's reach.

While Western missionaries facing trouble could retreat to safer shores, Brother D. and his family lived under the constant weight of surveillance, their every move watched, their every connection noted. Yet this very permanence of pressure became their most powerful testimony–living proof that God's truth cannot be contained by human restrictions or intimidated by earthly threats. Their daily endurance spoke louder than any sermon about the sustaining power of divine purpose.

Questions for Reflection:

- How does God transform our ordinary roles into extraordinary opportunities for His Kingdom?
- Where do you see divine creativity emerging through human pressure?
- What seemingly mundane aspects of our lives might God be wanting to use for His eternal purposes?

Points for Prayer:

- For those distributing God's Word in restricted nations, that their ordinary courage would yield extraordinary fruit
- For wisdom in discovering creative pathways for truth in pressured places
- For protection over believers living under constant surveillance
- For courage that grows stronger rather than weaker under threat
- For God's Word to find its way through every human barrier to hearts hungry for truth

Prayer Response:

Lord of hidden pathways, we stand in awe of how You weave eternal purposes through earthly limitations. Thank You for servants like Brother D. who show us how ordinary faithfulness becomes extraordinary impact in Your hands. Thank You for revealing how no human barrier can ultimately contain Your truth, no earthly threat intimidates Your purposes. Grant courage to those facing daily pressure for their faith, wisdom to those seeking creative ways to share Your Word, and protection to all who risk safety to spread Your message. May we, like Brother D., discover that pressure becomes a possibility when surrendered to Your purposes.

Bob Hare's Question:

Balancing Hunger and Eternity

━━

1980s

━━

"Man shall not live on bread alone, but on every
word that comes from the mouth of God."

MATTHEW 4:4

IN VIENNA, WHERE the intersection of physical and spiritual
need wrote daily stories of human struggle, Bob Hare posed a
question that cut to the heart of Christian mission: "Which is
more important–spiritual or physical hunger?" As millions of dollars
flowed into food relief programs while spiritual hunger remained
largely unfunded, his challenge echoed with prophetic resonance.

Bob Hare was not merely posing theoretical questions—he was a devoted missionary whose life embodied faithful service behind the Iron Curtain. As a key figure with EEM, his work focused specifically on providing Bibles and Christian literature to spiritually hungry people in communist-controlled regions. His ministry in Vienna positioned him at a strategic crossroads where he witnessed first-hand both the physical deprivation and spiritual starvation affecting millions during the Cold War era.

The poignancy of his question came from witnessing how readily the world mobilized for physical needs while spiritual hunger often went unaddressed. His deep commitment to Bible distribution throughout Eastern Europe made him intimately familiar with the transformative power of God's Word in regions where it was scarce and precious. This wasn't abstract theology for Bob. It was the daily reality of his calling as he worked to meet the profound spiritual hunger he encountered in his mission field.

The context of his question emerged from decades of witnessing both forms of hunger firsthand. "Today we are reading and hearing about great hunger in many places of the world," he observed. "Millions and millions of dollars are being sent by different nations, churches and organizations, some in the way of food and grain and some in currency."

Yet beneath this flow of physical aid lay a deeper question that haunted him: Why did the world mobilize so readily for physical hunger while spiritual starvation received comparatively little attention? This wasn't just philosophical musing—surveys showed that eighty percent of the world lacked access to Bibles, a statistic that Hare saw not just as data but as a tragedy demanding response.

His perspective wasn't born of detachment but emerged from years of practical ministry. Working with Eastern European churches, he had witnessed how spiritual nourishment often proved the catalyst for holistic transformation. "Do not get me wrong," he would say, careful to maintain balance. "I think we need to help people with their physical needs in order to help them with the spiritual. But which is more important?"

The question became particularly poignant when considering the origins of EEM itself–an organization founded and sustained specifically to address spiritual hunger. While others focused primarily on physical relief, EEM maintained its focus on providing "spiritual food," recognizing that while both were necessary, eternal sustenance carried unique significance.

When a plea arrived for 1,500 New Testaments for one of the countries in Eastern Europe, Hare saw it as more than just another request–it was a cry from souls hungry for truth. His response reflected the heart of his ministry: "How am I going to answer this plea? It will depend mostly on you, our friends."

Questions for Reflection:

- How do we balance meeting physical and spiritual needs in ministry?
- What role does spiritual nourishment play in holistic transformation?
- Where might we be overlooking spiritual hunger while addressing physical needs?

Points for Prayer:

- For wisdom in balancing physical and spiritual ministry
- For resources to meet both types of hunger
- For those lacking access to God's Word
- For hearts to recognize spiritual hunger as real hunger
- For generous response to both physical and spiritual needs

Prayer Response:

Lord of all provision, we thank You for servants like Bob Hare who help us wrestle with fundamental questions of ministry priority.

Thank You for those who recognize both physical and spiritual hunger as real needs requiring real response. Give us wisdom to balance these vital aspects of ministry, courage to address both forms of hunger, and generosity to respond to each need as it arises. Help us see beyond immediate physical needs to eternal spiritual hunger, while neglecting neither. May we, like Bob, maintain a clear vision of eternal priorities while serving present needs.

Hidden Faith:

When Cardinals Smuggle and Principals Preach

1980s

"The Kingdom of heaven is like treasure hidden in a field."

MATTHEW 13:44

THE VATICAN'S POWER extends to the furthest corners of the earth through 180 Cardinals who shape Catholic doctrine and policy. In Bosnia and Herzegovina, this influence resulted in decades of resistance to Protestant Bible distribution, until God chose to turn one Cardinal into His own courier.

I lean forward in my chair, hardly daring to breathe, as Jura describes the scene in the Cardinal's office. This isn't just another story of Bible distribution—it's a testament to how God can transform His fiercest opponents into His most effective agents.

"The Cardinal didn't just give permission," Jura tells me, his voice still carrying traces of amazement years later. "He became our smuggler."

In my years documenting stories of the persecuted church, I've heard countless tales of believers sneaking Bibles past authorities. But this was different. This time, God had directly chosen the authority figure himself.

The plan was audacious in its simplicity: The Cardinal would use his authority to move 60,000 Bibles into Bosnia and Herzegovina. No customs fees. No inspections. God's Word traveling under official protection.

"At every checkpoint," Jura continues, "the Cardinal himself would show his diplomatic passport. The same guards who might have seized our cargo simply waved us through. God had turned the system meant to control religion into His delivery service."

But this wasn't an isolated incident. Across Eastern Europe, God was orchestrating an underground revolution - not through traditional channels of persecution and resistance, but by transforming the very structures meant to contain His Word.

Consider Vladimir Skovorodnikov. In the frozen reaches of Siberia, this Communist school principal sat at his desk, haunted by questions his atheist training couldn't answer. Like Nicodemus coming to Jesus by night, Vladimir had secretly begun seeking truth beyond Marx and Lenin.

"The Party thought they were positioning a reliable Communist as Minister of Education," Mike Armour explains. "They had no idea they were installing God's chosen agent of transformation."

When Vladimir slipped into that teacher training session, watching American educators present character curriculum, he wasn't just a high-ranking official evaluating a program. He was a seeker about to encounter the God who had been pursuing him since those long nights in his arctic classroom.

"I knew whatever power controls the universe had put me there for a purpose," Vladimir would later confess. "I felt called to bring about a moral revolution." The irony is stunning–a Communist official dreaming of moral revolution, not knowing he was being drawn into God's revolutionary plan.

The scope of what followed still takes my breath away. Through Vladimir's position, God would plant His Word in schools across Siberia. The same educational system that had been used to indoctrinate generations in atheism became the vehicle for introducing children to Scripture.

But God wasn't finished. In a divine plot twist that reads like something from the Book of Acts, Vladimir himself would encounter Christ through the very book he had helped introduce to teach others. Standing in the baptistery in Dallas, this former Communist official publicly declared his allegiance to a different Kingdom.

Questions for Reflection:

- When have you seen God turn an opponent into an ally for His purposes?
- What position of influence has God given you that could be used for His Kingdom?
- Like Vladimir, what "impossible" transformation is God preparing in your sphere of influence?

Points for Prayer:

- For current government officials who are secretly seeking truth
- For believers in positions of authority to have wisdom and boldness

- For God to continue turning systems of opposition into channels of His Word
- For protection over those risking position and status to advance God's Kingdom

Prayer Response:

Lord, we marvel at how You turn opposition into opportunity, transforming hearts that once resisted Your truth into channels for Your grace. Give us courage to be Your agents of transformation wherever You've placed us, and help us see every position of influence as a platform for Your purposes. May we remember that no heart is too hardened, no system too entrenched, and no barrier too strong for Your transforming love.

Personal

Transformation

Stories

———

Oleg's Story:

Finding Light in Russia's Spiritual Void

1980s

*"My people are destroyed
for lack of knowledge."*

HOSEA 4:6

I N THE SPIRITUAL landscape of 1980s Russia, where decades of state atheism had created a profound hunger for truth, a young man named Oleg found himself caught in a quest for meaning. The nation stood at a crossroads, with whispers of change rippling through society as people began questioning the emptiness left by communist ideology.

"The great breakthrough came in the 80s," Oleg recalls, his voice carrying both the weight of memory and the lightness of redemption. Rumors spread about someone who might be a savior—or condemnation—for society. These mysterious discussions contained fragments of biblical knowledge, just enough to kindle curiosity in Oleg's searching heart.

"Someone said, well, it was foretold in some old good book, the Bible, that this person would come and he has a mark on his head," he remembers. This snippet of scriptural knowledge, however distorted, became the catalyst for a life-changing journey. "I was thinking, what is this Bible? Where can I find it?"

His quest led him to believers who did more than share their faith—they shared Scripture itself, placing in his hands the very book he had been seeking. "I finally met people who believed in Jesus Christ, and they gave me a free copy of the Bible," Oleg shares. That gift became the doorway to transformation as he immersed himself in its pages. "I came to Christ after reading for a year."

This personal awakening revealed a broader truth about his homeland. Across Russia, millions hungered for the same spiritual foundation he had discovered. "People are still in need to know the foundation, you know, the fundamentals of the Bible story," he observes with passionate conviction. "The void is great. I mean, just who is gonna fill that gap?"

God's answer to that question would eventually include Oleg himself as he leads efforts to provide Bibles and Bible based materials to people across these nations. His personal experience of receiving Scripture shapes his mission to ensure others have the same opportunity.

The sacred gift of God's Word continues to transform lives through the ministry he oversees. "When people begin to read, joy comes. Understanding comes and faith comes too," explains one partner working alongside him. The testimonies multiply—women in crisis finding hope, those struggling with addiction discovering freedom, communities being restored through access to Scripture.

For Oleg, the mission is personal, born from his own journey from darkness to light. "This idea of giving bibles to people was very dear to me because I received the Bible," he shares. His life stands as a testament to the power of Scripture to pierce even the darkest ideological void.

In the continuing story of Russia's spiritual awakening, Oleg plays his part with the passion of one who remembers what it means to search for truth and finally find it. "This is a great blessing to the country, to the people," he declares, "to find the hope to see and to open their eyes for the light that Jesus is giving them."

Questions for Reflection:

- What "spiritual voids" exist in your own society that need to be filled with biblical truth?
- How has your personal encounter with Scripture shaped your desire to share it with others?
- Like Oleg, where might God be calling you to help "fill the gap" for those seeking spiritual foundations?
- What barriers to biblical knowledge exist in your community, and how might they be overcome?

Points for Prayer:

- For continued open doors to distribute Bibles in Russia and Kazakhstan
- For protection and wisdom for Oleg and his team
- For those reading Scripture for the first time to encounter Christ

- For ministries partnering with EEM in these nations
- For the softening of hearts historically hardened by atheistic ideology

Prayer Response:

Lord of revelation, we thank You for Your Word that penetrates even the darkest ideological voids. Thank You for igniting curiosity in Oleg's heart through mere fragments of Scripture, and for the believers who placed Your Word in his seeking hands. We praise You for transforming him from seeker to servant, using his own journey to fuel ministry to others. Give protection to those distributing Bibles in Russia and Kazakhstan, and may each Scripture placed in hungry hands bring light where darkness has reigned. Help us recognize similar spiritual voids in our own communities and use us as vessels to fill those gaps with Your truth.

Victor's Redemption:

From Shadows to Shepherd

▬

1990s

▬

"For I will forgive their wickedness and
will remember their sins no more."

HEBREWS 8:12

I N THE SHADOW of Stalin's legacy, where German heritage became a sentence of suffering, a story of redemption was waiting to unfold. Victor's family narrative begins with a train journey to Siberia - his mother and two siblings forced into the stark reality of the gulags while German men were sentenced to coal mines. One sibling would never return, dying in that frozen wasteland. Yet from these ashes of family tragedy, Victor would be born after his mother's return to Ukraine - a new life in a land marked by his family's pain.

By the 1970s, Victor had become an instrument of the very system that had torn his family apart. As a Soviet security service policeman working in conjunction with the KGB, his duties were clear: locate religious gatherings, infiltrate them, spy on their activities, and file reports. Though his hands never directly arrested, shot, or sentenced anyone to the gulags, he carried the weight of knowing his reports led to such consequences. Each document he filed potentially sealed another believer's fate.

But God's redemptive power knows no bounds. In the 1990s, as the Soviet Union crumbled and Ukraine tasted freedom, Victor encountered Christ at a revival meeting. The same faith he had once worked to suppress now took root in his own heart. His transformation deepened when he discovered Sasha Prokopchuk's Bible program on television, leading him to attend church-planting seminars in the early 2000s.

Today, in a divine reversal that only God could orchestrate, Victor has planted four churches in his hometown area of Kryvyi Rih. The man who once reported on underground believers now builds congregations in the light of freedom. His life stands as a testament to Christ's power to transform not just individuals, but entire legacies of pain into platforms for His glory.

Questions for Reflection:

- How does Victor's story challenge our assumptions about who can be transformed by God?
- What does this narrative teach us about God's redemptive power?
- How might God be working in the lives of those who currently oppose His Kingdom?

Points for Prayer:

- For those currently involved in persecuting Christians
- For courage for believers ministering in restricted areas
- For more transformational testimonies like Victor's
- For the churches Victor has planted
- For healing of generational trauma from persecution

Prayer Response:

Merciful Father, we marvel at Your power to transform lives. Thank You for stories like Victor's that remind us no one is beyond Your reach. Give us faith to believe there can be transformation among those who oppose Your Kingdom today. Help us see beyond current roles and positions to the potential You see in every heart. Use us, like Victor, to build Your Kingdom in unexpected ways.

Sacred Whispers:

Igor's Journey from Secret Baptism to Kingdom Builder in Russia

1990s

"Remember your word to your servant, for you have given me hope. My comfort in my suffering is this: Your promise preserves my life."

PSALM 119:49-50

I N THE SHADOW of Soviet atheism, where faith was forbidden and believers risked persecution, an elderly grandmother performed a sacred act of rebellion. With trembling hands and whispered prayers, she secretly baptized her grandson Igor, planting seeds of faith in soil that the Communist regime had tried to render barren. As water trickled over the child's forehead, she whispered the Lord's Prayer in ancient Church Slavic, words that would echo in Igor's heart long after her voice had faded from this world.

This clandestine baptism remained a buried treasure in Igor's life, hidden beneath layers of state-sanctioned atheism. On the surface, he grew up as the system demanded—a good Soviet citizen, educated in materialistic philosophy and scientific atheism. Yet deep within, something inexplicable stirred—an innate sense that there was more to existence than what his textbooks proclaimed, more than what Party officials declared in their strident speeches.

The dormant seeds his grandmother had planted lay waiting for the right season, the right moment for divine germination. That moment arrived in the form of a roommate named Samuel, whose quiet faith proved more compelling than years of atheistic indoctrination. One evening, as shadows lengthened across their shared space, Samuel shared the simple yet profound story of Jesus—not as distant mythology but as living reality.

"I realized in that moment," Igor would later recount, "that God wasn't just some abstract concept to debate. He was a Person seeking a relationship with me. The Jesus that Samuel described knew my name, knew my thoughts, knew the longing that I couldn't explain even to myself."

This revelation shattered the carefully constructed walls of Igor's Soviet worldview. The personal God that Samuel described awakened memories of his grandmother's whispered prayers, creating a bridge between his hidden past and possible future. Where Communist ideology had offered only collective identity, the Gospel offered personal invitation. Where the state demanded allegiance through fear, Christ extended a personal relationship through love.

Igor's hunger for spiritual truth grew insatiable. When EEM

presented him with a Bible—a treasure nearly impossible to find in those days—Igor consumed its words with the intensity of a man who had been starving without recognizing his hunger. He marveled at the New Testament's simplicity and depth, finding in its pages both the wisdom his mind sought and the relationship his heart craved.

The waters that had touched him in secret as a child now called to him again. In a powerful act of reclaiming his true identity, Igor was baptized publicly embracing the faith his grandmother had only dared to whisper. The circle that began with her secret act of devotion found completion in his open declaration of faith.

Yet Igor's story was just beginning. With Bibles and theological resources provided by EEM—treasures rarer than gold in post-Soviet Russia—he gathered a small community of believers. What started as quiet conversations over open Scriptures grew into the first officially recognized Church of Christ school in Russia, a development that would have seemed impossible just years before.

Igor's ministry expanded beyond what anyone could have imagined. The partnership with EEM bore fruit in published theological resources, new congregations, and countless lives transformed by the Gospel. The seeds planted in secrecy by his grandmother had grown into a harvest that nourished many.

Today, Igor looks back in wonder at the thread of divine purpose woven through his life. From a secret baptism performed under the shadow of oppression to an officially recognized ministry bringing light to many, his journey testifies to how God preserves faith even in the most hostile environments. The prayer his grandmother whispered in Church Slavic now rises openly from congregations he helped establish, echoing across generations and political systems, bearing witness to a God who works in quiet corners to change the course of history.

In the end, Igor's story reminds us that no government, no

ideology, no system of oppression can ultimately prevent the growth of what God has planted. Though the seeds may lie dormant for decades, waiting for the right conditions, they remain alive—ready to burst forth when divine timing meets human openness. The faith whispered by his grandmother found its voice in Igor's ministry, proving that sometimes the most powerful revolutions begin not with manifestos and marches, but with a grandmother's prayer.

Questions for Reflection:

- What "seeds of faith" were planted in your early life that you may not have recognized at the time?
- Like Igor's grandmother, how might your faithfulness today impact generations beyond your knowledge?
- When have you experienced a moment of spiritual awakening similar to Igor's conversation with Samuel?
- What resources or mentors has God brought into your life at critical moments of spiritual growth?
- Where in your life have you seen God's timing transform what seemed like a disadvantage into an opportunity for ministry?

Points for Prayer:

- For the elderly believers in restrictive societies who keep faith alive through quiet acts of devotion
- For those serving in evangelistic roles like Samuel, whose simple sharing of Jesus can transform lives
- For ministries providing Bibles and resources in regions where they remain scarce
- For Christian educators establishing schools and training programs in formerly atheistic societies
- For the next generation of leaders being shaped by mentors like Prentice Meador and Igor

Prayer Response:

Faithful God, we marvel at Your patient work across generations—how a grandmother's whispered prayer became a grandson's public ministry. Thank You for preserving faith in hostile soil. We pray for those secretly nurturing belief in restrictive places, that their courage would bear fruit beyond their imagining. Strengthen those providing Bibles where they remain rare. Help us recognize the seeds You've planted in our own lives, waiting for the right season to grow. In Jesus' name, who makes all things new in His time. Amen.

From Soviet Captain to Kingdom Captain:

Igor's Transformation

___

1990s

___

"For the message of the cross is foolishness to those who are perishing, but to us who are being saved it is the power of God."

1 CORINTHIANS 1:18

The Warrior's Conversion

THE COLD HALLS of Soviet military authority had shaped Igor Kovolov's mind for fifteen years. As an Air Force Captain, he embodied the atheistic ideals of the regime, his worldview constructed from the sturdy bricks of Communist doctrine and sealed with the mortar of materialistic philosophy. Each day served to reinforce the walls between Igor and faith, between certainty and mystery, between atheism and God.

In 1989, as the winds of change began to sweep across Eastern Europe, Igor stood just six months from military retirement and the lifetime pension that would follow. But history had other plans. The Soviet Union collapsed, and with it, Igor's financial security vanished overnight. The Captain who had devoted his life to the system found himself cast adrift in a newly independent Ukraine, struggling alongside his mother Inessa to build a life amid the rubble of failed ideology.

The hard soil of Igor's heart had been broken by circumstance, but it had not yet been prepared for planting. When he learned that Christians from South Carolina would be holding a two-week evangelistic campaign in Luhansk in 1993, Igor saw not an opportunity for spiritual growth but a battlefield for intellectual combat. Each day, he arrived armed with arguments, ready to publicly debate the teacher and prove that atheism stood on firmer ground than Christianity.

Yet something unexpected happened in those exchanges. Like Saul on the road to Damascus, Igor found himself confronted not just by words but by Presence. The logic he had wielded as a weapon began to crumble in his hands, revealing a deeper truth beneath. By the end of the two weeks, the Soviet Captain felt his heart changing, softening under the gentle rain of grace.

"I eventually had to give in to the logic of God existing and loving me," Igor would later explain, his voice still carrying traces of wonder at the transformation. In divine irony that only the Author of redemption could script, the man who came to argue against faith was baptized by the very Christian he had debated so fiercely. The warrior who had served an empire built on atheism now pledged allegiance to the King of Kings.

Igor's conversion rippled outward. Soon, his mother Inessa also embraced the faith, and the South Carolina church that had sent missionaries established a congregation in Luhansk, Ukraine. In perfect poetic harmony, the former atheist became its preacher, while his mother served as custodian. The military captain had found a new commission in God's army.

Yet the story was not complete. For years, Igor tried to hold Christian activities in local schools where he taught Computer Science and English, only to face constant rejection. Principals deemed such activities too risky in a culture still emerging from decades of religious suppression. But God was writing a larger narrative.

As EEM built relationships with education officials across Ukraine, something remarkable happened. The very Ministry of Education in Luhansk that once embodied Soviet atheism now requested Bibles for its schools. Doors that had been firmly closed to Igor suddenly swung open, allowing him to freely share God's Word in classrooms throughout the region.

This profound transformation—from Soviet military captain to captain in the Lord's army—stands as a testament to God's power to redeem not just individuals but entire systems. Igor had lost his pension but gained an eternal inheritance. He had surrendered his atheistic certainty but discovered a deeper truth. And in perfect Kingdom mathematics, what seemed like subtraction had become multiplication as more hearts opened to the Gospel through his ministry.

Today, Igor continues his work in Luhansk, boldly sharing the Good News with people who, like him, are emerging from darkness into light. His story reminds us that no heart is too hardened, no mind too indoctrinated, no soul too distant for God's transforming grace. The Captain who once defended atheism now stands as living proof of the power of Christ to make all things new.

Questions for Reflection:

- Like Igor, have you ever clung to beliefs or ideologies that later proved incomplete or untrue? How did God guide you to a fuller understanding?
- Where in your life have you experienced apparent loss (like Igor's pension) that God later transformed into spiritual gain?
- What "doors" in your sphere of influence seem firmly closed to the Gospel? How might God be preparing to open them in ways you can't yet imagine?
- Igor debated Christians before becoming one himself. How might God be using the questions and challenges of skeptics in your life to ultimately draw them to Himself?
- In what ways are you using your professional position (as Igor does with his teaching) to create opportunities to share Christ with others?

Points for Prayer:

- For former military personnel and government officials in post-Communist nations who are searching for truth beyond the ideologies they once served
- For educators in Eastern Europe who face difficult decisions about allowing spiritual content in their classrooms
- For the continued work of Igor, Inessa, and the Luhansk church as they minister in challenging circumstances
- For those who are currently debating and arguing against Christianity, that like Igor, they might encounter the living Christ through their questions
- For courage among believers working in secular educational environments around the world

Prayer Response:

Lord of unexpected transformations, we stand in awe of how You turned an atheist military captain into a proclaimer of Your Gospel. Thank You that no heart is beyond Your reach. We pray for those who, like Igor once did, oppose Your truth—may their questions lead them to You. Turn what seems like loss into Kingdom purpose. Open doors that appear permanently closed, and empower believers in education and government who face opposition when sharing their faith. Protect Igor, Inessa, and the church in Luhansk as they continue serving as testimonies to Your transforming grace.

Faina's Freedom:

From Prison to a Life of Ministry

▬

2 0 0 0 s

▬

"Then you will know the truth, and the truth will set you free."

JOHN 8:32

I N THE STARK corridors of a Kazakhstani prison, where steel
bars cast long shadows across young lives, God was orchestrating a story of redemption through the most unexpected of
currencies: soap, toothpaste, and memorized Scripture. For fifteen-
year-old Faina, whose path to these cold halls had been paved with
family tragedy - one brother lost to suicide, another to imprisonment–divine grace would prove both practical and profound.

The missionaries' strategy seemed almost too simple: offer basic necessities in exchange for memorized verses. Yet in God's way of managing resources, even the humblest transactions can become channels of transforming truth. Faina began learning verses, not understanding their meaning but treasuring the simple dignity found in clean teeth and washed hands. Each word memorized planted seeds in soil that loss had made fertile for hope.

The turning point came through John 3:16. As she worked to explain these words about divine love, something broke open in her heart. The girl who had started memorizing Scripture for soap found herself weeping over truth that no earthly commodity could purchase. "Jesus died for me!" she proclaimed to the missionaries, her voice carrying the weight of genuine revelation.

But God wasn't finished writing her story of redemption. The same missionaries who had traded toiletries for truth now invested in her freedom, paying for her release. In His divine narrative, even prison became preparation for purpose. At nineteen, Faina married Ruslan, and together they began ministering to youth throughout Central Asia, sharing the transformative power of God's Word that had first reached her through such humble means.

Today, Ruslan and Faina continue their work with young people across Central Asia, passionate about sharing the power of God's Word that so dramatically changed Faina's own life. Their story stands as a testament to how God can use the simplest acts of kindness to plant seeds of eternal transformation.

Questions for Reflection:

- How does God use our basic needs as pathways to deeper spiritual truth?
- What "simple transactions" in our own lives might God be using for eternal purposes?

- How can practical ministry open doors for profound spiritual transformation?

Points for Prayer:
- For young people in prison systems worldwide to encounter God's Word
- For wisdom in combining practical help with spiritual truth
- For creative strategies in reaching those in confined circumstances
- For the multiplication of testimonies like Faina's
- For those currently ministering in prison systems

Prayer Response:
Master of redemption's story, we marvel at how You use the simplest things—soap, memorized verses, acts of kindness—to plant seeds of eternal transformation. Thank You for servants willing to enter difficult places with both practical help and eternal truth. We pray for those currently in prisons, that like Faina, they might discover Your love through unexpected means. Grant wisdom to those ministering in challenging environments, creativity in sharing Your Word, and multiplication of every seed planted in confined spaces. May we, like those missionaries, learn to see how everyday needs can become gateways to eternal truth.

Lida's Awakening:

From Asylum to Authentic Faith

2003

*"Therefore, if anyone is in Christ, the new creation
has come: The old has gone, the new is here!"*

2 CORINTHIANS 5:17

WHEN LIDA FLED Iran for Austria in 2003, she
carried with her the weight of an abusive marriage
and two sons who needed protection. God was the
furthest thing from her mind—a distant concept she believed

had no interest in her life. Her path to faith would begin with an act of pragmatic deception that God would transform into genuine revelation.

Seeking asylum, Lida received practical advice: become a Christian to strengthen her refugee application. She followed through, receiving baptism and a certificate from a Catholic church without understanding its meaning. The certificate secured her refugee status, but left her spiritual life unchanged.

Everything shifted when another refugee invited her to a Persian Christian church service. Arriving early, she encountered something unexpected–worship team members rehearsing songs about God. Tears filled her eyes as she realized people could actually sing to God. This simple discovery cracked open her heart to possibilities she had never imagined.

The pivotal moment came when she confronted the man who had advised her to get baptized: "How can I be a Christian? I don't even have a Bible!" His response was unconventional–digging through his cluttered apartment, underneath his couch cushions, through scattered trash, until he extracted a Bible. "Out of the trash came treasure," Lida would later say. "And it saved my life."

Today, Lida wears a cross not as an empty symbol but as a conversation starter. "I have caught many fish now," she says with joy. She hosts two Bible studies weekly, first inviting people to language studies, then naturally transitioning to spiritual discussions as relationships develop. The woman who once sought only a certificate now leads others to authentic faith.

Questions for Reflection:

- How does God sometimes use our imperfect motives to lead us to genuine faith?
- What role does authentic worship play in opening hearts to God?

- How can practical needs become doorways to spiritual transformation?
- What are the other symbols we use to convey our beliefs/ values to others?

Points for Prayer:

- For refugees seeking both physical and spiritual sanctuary
- For those holding empty religious certifications to find living faith
- For Bible study leaders working with immigrant communities
- For those using language studies as bridges to share faith
- For protection of believers who still travel to restricted countries

Prayer Response:

Father of all nations, we thank You for Your patience in drawing people to genuine faith, even when they begin with imperfect motives. Thank You for testimonies like Lida's that remind us nothing is wasted in Your economy of grace. Help us recognize the treasure of Your Word, even when it comes from unexpected places. Use us to guide others from empty religion to living relationship with You.

Worth Everything:

Elena's Unshakable Faith

2010s

"Be joyful in hope, patient in affliction,
faithful in prayer."

ROMANS 12:12

IN THE MIST-SHROUDED hills of Transylvania, Romania, where ancient traditions and communist shadows still lingered, God was writing a story of luminous courage through a young girl named Elena. Her journey began not with dramatic revelation but with simple English lessons from Anne Boyd, a missionary widow in her seventies who had chosen to remain in

Romania despite her family's desperate pleas after her husband's death. "What do you mean, come home?" Anne would respond. "I am home."

Using a children's Bible as their textbook, Anne taught far more than language. As weeks of lessons transformed into months of quiet discipleship, Elena found herself drawn not just to new words, but to the sacred stories between the covers. One afternoon, watching Anne pray with a familiarity that spoke of deep relationship rather than religious obligation, Elena's voice broke the silence: "I wish I could pray like that."

"You can," Anne assured her, the certainty in her voice carrying decades of tested faith.

Elena's eyes filled with shadows beyond her years. "No," she whispered, "I've done horrible things. God would never want to hear from me."

Anne's weathered hand covered the girl's trembling fingers. "Oh, Elena," she replied, her voice gentle yet unwavering, "God wants to hear from you more than you can possibly imagine."

This holy invitation became the doorway through which divine grace would flood a wounded heart. Like the disciples before her who recognized their spiritual poverty, Elena made the most transformative request possible: "Teach me to pray." In the sanctuary of Anne's patient presence, she began a hesitant conversation with a God she was only beginning to know, eventually revealing the darkest shadow in her young life—horrific abuse at the hands of her father that had convinced her she was beyond love's reach.

When Elena declared her desire to follow Jesus, Anne baptized her in a small bathtub—a sacred ceremony performed in whispers. But secrets in close communities rarely remain hidden. Upon discovering his daughter's conversion, her father flew into a rage so violent that Elena nearly died from the beating. Anne, explicitly forbidden from contact, nevertheless sneaked into the hospital, where she prayed with the young believer whose faith was being forged in fire rather than theory.

Three years later, at seventeen, Elena sat before visitors documenting testimonies from behind the former Iron Curtain. As she recounted her story, tears streamed down her face—not tears of self-pity, but of wonder at being found worthy of God's love. The director, struck by the cost of her discipleship, asked the question that cut to the heart of faith: "Was there ever a point where you thought following Jesus wasn't worth it? You've been beaten, rejected, ostracized... did you ever reach a breaking point?"

Elena's response came without a moment's hesitation, her eyes suddenly clear and voice steady: "Oh no, no, no. He is worth everything." The simplicity and certainty of her declaration silenced the room.

Then, looking directly into the camera as if addressing countless unseen seekers, she added words that would later reduce even the documentary's seasoned videographer to tears: "If you're watching this and seeking God, just keep looking. Because when you find Him, you'll know—you'll never let Him go.

The documentary team—seasoned professionals who had interviewed hundreds of believers across Eastern Europe—found themselves overwhelmed, unable to maintain professional detachment in the face of such raw, tested faith. The director later confessed he could barely speak, while the cameraman admitted he had completely abandoned his technical focus, caught up in the holy moment unfolding before him.

In the years that followed, Elena's story continued to unfold in ways that testified to grace's transforming power. She married a Christian man and welcomed a child into the world. But perhaps most astonishing was her response when asked about her relationship with her abusive father. With the same steady gaze that had declared Christ's supreme worth, she replied: "We're striving to study the Bible with him right now."

Elena's testimony challenges our comfortable Christianity with devastating precision. Through her unwavering declaration that Christ is "worth everything," we glimpse authentic discipleship not as inspirational theory but as lived reality—a faith that has counted the cost and still chosen Jesus, a love strong enough to pursue reconciliation with the very one who inflicted the deepest wounds. Her life stands as both invitation and challenge: What would we endure for the One who endured everything for us?

Questions for Reflection:

- Where in your life are you hesitating to fully commit to Christ because of potential cost?
- How does Elena's statement "He is worth everything" challenge your assessment of Christ's value?
- What might be keeping you from believing God wants to hear your prayers?
- How might God be calling you to be "Jesus" to someone as Anne was to Elena?

Points for Prayer:

- For believers facing family rejection and abuse for their faith
- For missionaries who remain faithful in difficult fields despite personal cost
- For those who feel too damaged to approach God in prayer
- For mentoring relationships that bridge generations and reveal Christ's love
- For reconciliation between persecutors and those they have harmed

Prayer Response:

Lord of transforming value, we stand humbled before testimonies like Elena's that expose the comfortable calculations of our own faith.

Thank You for showing us what wholehearted devotion truly looks like. Forgive us for the times we've counted the cost and found it too high. Help us recognize Your surpassing worth, that we might declare with conviction: "You are worth everything." Grant courage to those facing persecution, wisdom to those mentoring new believers, and healing to those who cannot yet believe You want to hear their prayers. May we, like Anne, demonstrate Your love to those who need it most, and like Elena, hold fast to You regardless of the cost. Amen.

Galena's Leap of Faith:

Breaking the Chains of Atheism

——

2010s

——

*"For it is God who works in you
to will and to act in order to
fulfill his good purpose."*

PHILIPPIANS 2:13

I N THE RURAL state of Luhansk, Ukraine, where the echoes
of Soviet ideology still lingered in school hallways, an unexpected transformation was taking place. Galena, an energetic
education administrator, welcomed visitors into her office with
animated conversation and genuine hospitality. Yet beneath her

passionate exterior lay a story of deep skepticism born from decades of Communist propaganda.

When boxes of Children's Bibles arrived at her school, Galena's first instinct was born from years of conditioning. "These free Bibles must be part of some scheme," she thought, memories of past propaganda fueling her suspicion. With meticulous determination, she began examining every single box, searching for hidden agendas between the pages.

What she discovered instead was something far more profound—truth in its purest form. As she finished her inspection, tears welling in her eyes, Galena's voice trembled with emotion: "These are just Bibles! Thank you! Thank you!" But it was her next words that captured seven decades of spiritual hunger: "We have been trying to escape atheism for seventy years, and now you are freeing us to teach our children about God."

In that moment, years of state-imposed atheism crumbled before the simple power of God's Word. Galena's transformation from skeptic to advocate symbolized a deeper change taking place across Eastern Europe—a region awakening from decades of spiritual suppression.

Her story reminds us that sometimes the greatest barriers to faith aren't physical walls but the invisible ones built by years of systematic unbelief. Yet even these can fall when confronted with the authentic power of God's Word.

Questions for Reflection:

- How do our past experiences and conditioning affect our ability to receive truth?
- What "invisible walls" might be preventing us from fully embracing God's Word?
- How can we help others overcome skepticism born from past hurts or propaganda?

Points for Prayer:

- For educators and administrators in formerly atheistic regions
- For wisdom in presenting God's Word to those conditioned against it
- For healing from the lasting effects of anti-religious propaganda
- For courage to embrace truth despite past conditioning
- For the next generation being taught about God for the first time

Prayer Response:

Lord of all truth, we thank You for Your patient work in hearts long closed to Your Word. Thank You for faithful servants like Galena who, despite years of conditioning, remained open to Your transforming truth. Help us recognize and dismantle the invisible walls in our own hearts that keep us from fully embracing Your Word. Grant us wisdom and grace as we share Your truth with others who may be skeptical.

Masoud's Miracle:

From Drowning to Discipleship

▬

2010s

▬

"When you pass through the waters, I will be with you;
and through the rivers, they shall not overwhelm you."

ISAIAH 43:2

I N THE INK-BLACK waters off the coast of Lesbos, Greece, where ancient rocks have witnessed centuries of human struggle, a father's desperate prayer was about to become a testament to God's sovereign grace. The wooden boat that carried Masoud and his family, already riding dangerously low with its precious cargo of refugee souls, struck an unseen rock in the darkness. In that moment, as splintering wood gave way to churning waves, a journey toward physical safety became a pathway to eternal salvation.

Masoud's arms, which had moments before cradled his infant son, now grasped at empty water. Each dive into the dark sea brought increasing desperation. "I couldn't feel him," Masoud would later recall, his voice still carrying traces of that night's terror. "I was feeling all over, but I couldn't find him." Between dives, he could see his wife and daughter bobbing in their life jackets, illuminated by the flicker of a shoreline fire that seemed to mock their predicament.

It was in these depths, where human capability reaches its end, that Masoud found himself crying out to a God he barely knew. "What are you doing to me?" he pleaded beneath the waves. "I'm trying to get my family to a safe place. I heard your call, and I'm making this move. I'll do whatever you want—just please, save my son." The prayer carried all the raw honesty of a soul stripped bare by circumstance.

When he surfaced again, a shout cut through the chaos. There, atop the intact front section of the broken boat, lay his baby boy. The scene that followed seemed choreographed by divine providence: a Christian nurse waiting on shore, complete with stethoscope and warm blankets, ready to receive and revive the child who had been miraculously preserved.

But God wasn't finished writing this story. In the months that followed, Masoud found himself haunted by dreams. "Jesus wouldn't let me sleep," he explained with a gentle smile. "He kept coming to me, saying 'I'm Yeshua. You need to know me.'" The dreams persisted until Masoud finally received a Bible in his own language, where he discovered the Jesus of Scripture was the same one who had been pursuing him in his dreams.

Years later, when asked if Jesus still appeared in his dreams, Masoud's response revealed the beautiful progression of faith: "No," he said thoughtfully. "Now I see Him in you and you in him, and

He speaks through His Word. I hear something every day." The man who had once bargained with an unknown God in desperate waters had found that same God faithfully present in Scripture and community.

Questions for Reflection:
- When have you experienced God's presence most powerfully in times of crisis?
- How has God used dreams or unexpected means to draw you closer to Himself?
- Where do you see God's hand in the current refugee movements around the world?

Points for Prayer:
- For refugees making dangerous journeys seeking safety
- For those receiving supernatural revelations of Jesus
- For new believers transitioning from dreams to Scripture
- For protection of refugee families
- For more workers to help refugees encounter Christ

Prayer Response:
Father of all nations, who makes paths through the sea and speaks to seeking hearts in dreams, we stand in awe of Your persistent love. Thank You for using even the darkest moments as gateways to Your light. Give us eyes to see Your work in the refugee crisis, and hearts ready to welcome those You are drawing to Yourself. Help us be faithful witnesses to those You are pursuing through dreams and divine appointments.

Yasser and Zahra:

Love Stronger Than Tradition

2010s

"There is neither Jew nor Greek,
slave nor free, male nor female,
for you are all one in Christ Jesus."

GALATIANS 3:28

I N A SMALL refugee apartment in Greece, where the weight of centuries-old traditions hung heavy in the air, a Christian New Testament lay by Zahra's bedside like a quiet revolution. When her husband Yasser discovered it, the scene that unfolded could have been lifted from countless similar moments across generations of religious conflict. His words carried the thunder of 1,500 years of cultural conditioning: "You either get rid of this, or I have to kill you or divorce you."

In their Afghan culture, such threats weren't mere words. Divorce meant more than the end of a marriage—it meant social death, the severing of every community tie that gave a woman's life meaning and protection. Death, whether by honor killing or abandonment, loomed as a very real possibility. Yet in that pivotal moment, Zahra's response carried neither defiance nor fear. She simply said, "I can't."

Something in her gentle but immovable answer pierced Yasser's certainty. Later, finding himself alone with the forbidden book, he decided to read it himself—not seeking truth, but ammunition to prove it false. "The words and the text consumed me," he would later recall, his voice soft with wonder. "I couldn't put it down." Page after page, the Jesus he encountered defied his preconceptions, challenging not just his beliefs but the very foundations of his identity.

The transformation that followed would ripple far beyond their small family. Today, Yasser and Zahra lead a thriving church plant reaching out to Afghan refugees, their story a living testament to Christ's power to heal the deepest wounds of culture and tradition. In a beautiful display of divine irony, the man who once threatened death over a Bible now baptizes new believers, his hands offering life instead of judgment.

Their story challenges our assumptions about what's possible in our divided world. While diplomats and politicians seek peace through treaties and negotiations, Yasser and Zahra's journey demonstrates that true reconciliation—whether between husband and wife or between ancient enemies—flows from an encounter with Jesus. Their lives prove that no tradition is too entrenched, no divide too ancient, no heart too hardened for Christ's transforming love.

Questions for Reflection:

- What cultural or religious traditions might be keeping you from fully embracing God's truth?
- How has God turned opponents into allies in your own faith journey?
- Where do you see opportunities for Christ's love to heal ancient divisions in your community?

Points for Prayer:

- For couples divided by faith and tradition
- For more transformations among those opposed to the Gospel
- For church plants reaching refugees
- For healing of ancient religious conflicts
- For courage for believers from Muslim backgrounds

Prayer Response:

Sovereign Lord, who breaks down dividing walls of hostility, we praise You for Your power to transform hearts hardened by centuries of tradition. Thank You for showing us through Yasser and Zahra that no barrier is too high, no division too deep for Your love to overcome. Give us courage to stand firm in our faith while extending grace to those who oppose it. Help us be agents of Your reconciling love in our divided world.

Reconciled Brothers:

A Shia-Sunni Journey to Unity

2010s

---

*"For he himself is our peace, who has
made the two groups one."*

EPHESIANS 2:14

H IGH ABOVE ATHENS' ancient streets, where the
Acropolis bears silent witness to centuries of human division and reconciliation, God was writing a new chapter
of unity in an unlikely setting. In a converted upper room where
hundreds of Middle Eastern refugees gathered weekly for meals,
the aroma of spaghetti mingled with the fragrance of grace as two

men from Afghanistan demonstrated the transformative power of Christ's love.

Massoud and Yasser moved through the bustling space with infectious joy, their playful pasta-tossing and shared laughter echoing off walls that overlooked millennia of human conflict below. To casual observers, they appeared simply as two friends serving their fellow refugees. But their story carried weight far beyond that commanding view of Athens' historical heights.

"Were you friends back in Afghanistan?" The question sparked a response that pierced straight to the heart of divine reconciliation. Massoud's eyes held both memory and marvel as he replied, "Oh no! I am Shia. He is Sunni. In my country, we were mortal enemies. But in Jesus, we are brothers."

In that simple declaration lay the answer to a question that has confounded diplomats and peacemakers for generations: What has the power to break down the walls of a 1500-year-old holy war? Not a new ambassador. Not another peace treaty. The answer stood before them in flesh and blood – two former enemies now bound together by something stronger than ancient hatred.

From that elevated perch above Athens, where history's greatest philosophers once pondered humanity's deepest divisions, these two men demonstrated daily how the love of Christ transcends every barrier we construct. Their story represents more than individual salvation; it testifies to the gospel's unique power to heal wounds that political solutions cannot touch.

Their shared service to fellow refugees, their unity forged in exile, became a living parable—proving that in Christ, even the deepest religious and ethnic divisions dissolve into brotherhood. Their laughter rising above Athens' ancient stones echoes with prophetic significance—a glimpse of God's Kingdom breaking into our broken world.

Questions for Reflection:

- What "ancient divides" in our own communities need Christ's reconciling power?
- How does serving together break down barriers between people?
- What role can shared faith play in healing historical wounds?

Points for Prayer:

- For reconciliation between historical enemies in conflict zones
- For refugee communities finding unity in Christ
- For more testimonies of divine reconciliation across religious divides
- For church communities welcoming people from diverse backgrounds
- For the courage to love those we once considered enemies

Prayer Response:

Prince of Peace, we marvel at Your power to transform ancient enemies into beloved brothers. Thank You for testimonies like Massoud and Yasser's that remind us no divide is too deep for Your reconciling love. Help us see beyond historical barriers to recognize our shared humanity and potential brotherhood in Christ. Use us as instruments of Your peace in a world still divided by ancient hatreds.

Prison Walls to Open Hearts:

Brother CC8's Mission

2015

*"Remember those in prison as if
you were together with them."*

HEBREWS 13:3

I
N THE STARK confines of a Greek prison, where hope often
withers like flowers in winter, God was cultivating an unexpected garden of grace. The story begins not with a minister's
calling, but with a prisoner's cell number: CC8. It was here, in 1999,

that Patrick Usifo first encountered the Word that would transform not just his life, but the lives of countless others behind bars.

For Patrick, church was initially nothing more than a joke, the laughter of skepticism echoing off cold prison walls. But then came the gift—a Bible from an unknown sender, arriving like a seed carried on divine winds. In the endless hours of confinement, boredom became the unlikely midwife to revelation. He read the entire Bible in a week, then again, and again, each reading digging deeper furrows in the soil of his soul.

"God's Word has power to change people," Patrick would later testify, his own transformation becoming living proof of this truth. Over his fifteen-year sentence, what began as one man's encounter with Scripture blossomed into active Bible studies, his cell becoming a sanctuary where other inmates discovered the freedom that transcends physical constraints.

But God's story was far from finished. Upon his release in 2015, Patrick faced what seemed an insurmountable barrier—Greek law prohibited former inmates from returning to prison unless they committed another crime. Yet he felt called to return, not as a prisoner, but as a minister to those still bound. In an extraordinary display of divine intervention, his application for prison ministry received swift approval, defying all expectations.

Today, Patrick, known to inmates as Brother CC8, ministers in a prison system where only about thirty percent of prisoners are Greek nationals. His personal journey from skeptic to believer, from inmate to minister, gives him unique credibility with those he serves. He shares his story and relates to other prisoners through the very number that once defined his confinement—CC8 has become a symbol not of imprisonment, but of God's transforming power.

Through social media platforms and Greek Christian radio, his biblical teachings reach millions beyond prison walls. The man who once mocked faith now stands as a living testament to how God can transform a prison sentence into preparation for ministry, a cell number into a badge of honor in God's Kingdom.

Questions for Reflection:
- How does God use seasons of confinement to prepare us for future ministry?
- What "impossible" barriers might God be preparing to break down in our lives?
- How can our past struggles become platforms for sharing God's transforming power?

Points for Prayer:
- For current inmates discovering God's Word
- For former prisoners called to ministry
- For prison chaplains and volunteers worldwide
- For miraculous opening of doors for ministry
- For the multiplication of transformation stories in unlikely places

Prayer Response:
Master of transformation, we marvel at Your ability to turn prison cells into training grounds for ministry. Thank You for testimonies like Brother CC8's that remind us no life is beyond Your redemptive touch, no barrier too high for Your purposes. Grant us faith to believe for impossible breakthroughs, courage to return to difficult places as agents of Your grace, and wisdom to use our past struggles as bridges to reach others. May every number assigned by human systems become a testament to Your transforming power.

Former Foes,
United in Christ:
Serbian-Croatian Reconciliation

---

2 0 1 0 s

---

*"Be kind and compassionate to one another, forgiving
each other, just as in Christ God forgave you."*

EPHESIANS 4:32

THE COFFEE SHOP at Johnson Space Center buzzed with typical Houston morning chatter. But the conversation at one table was anything but typical. Despite their nations' history of bitter warfare, a Croatian and a Serbian colleague from

EEM sat sharing coffee and speaking the same language. An American businessman at the next table watched in bewilderment. "Wait a minute," he interrupted, recognizing their accents. "Why are you two sitting here together?"

The question hung in the air, heavy with the weight of history. Just years before, these men had worn different uniforms, carried different weapons, and fought on opposite sides of a war that tore the Balkans apart. Now they sat together, planning Bible distribution strategies.

Jura, EEM's Director for Central Europe, turned to the American with a smile that spoke of divine irony. "Because Jesus sits between us."

I've documented countless stories of persecution and reconciliation across the world, but this one stops me in my tracks. This isn't just about former enemies finding common ground—it's about God's power to transform combat veterans into Kingdom collaborators.

"I served in the Croatian Army for twenty-three years," Jura tells me, his military bearing still evident. "Drasko, EEM's Representative in Serbia, was in the Serbian forces. By human logic, we should be enemies. But God's math is different!"

Today, these former adversaries coordinate massive Bible distribution efforts across their respective territories. Where tanks once crossed borders bringing destruction, trucks now cross carrying God's Word. The same detailed knowledge of territory that once served military purposes now serves the Kingdom of God.

"We understand something profound now," Drasko explains, his voice carrying the weight of hard-won wisdom. "Jesus is the only one who can give our people peace. And in the Balkans, where the wars have been, this is a very important message."

The American businessman listens, transfixed, as they explain their work. His next question cuts to the heart: "But how? How do you get past all that history?"

Jura's answer is simple but profound: "We realized we were fighting the wrong war. The real battle isn't Croat versus Serb. It's darkness versus light. And in that war, we're on the same side."

Their partnership has opened doors that would remain firmly closed to outsiders. When Jura approaches Catholic leaders in Croatia, he comes as one who understands their culture and traditions. When Drasko works with Orthodox authorities in Serbia, he speaks their language—both literally and figuratively.

"Sometimes God's greatest victories come through former enemies," Jura reflects. "Who better to demonstrate the power of reconciliation than those who once aimed weapons at each other?"

Their story stands as a testament to God's ability to not just end conflicts, but to transform them into channels for His purposes. The very divisions that once separated them now serve as bridges for God's Word to cross.

At a recent EEM event in Houston, these brothers in Christ stood together, sharing their testimony. The gathered crowd witnessed something more powerful than a peace treaty—they saw living proof that in Christ, the deepest wounds can become the widest doors for God's work.

Questions for Reflection:

- What "enemy" in your life might God be calling you to reconcile with for His purposes?
- How could your past conflicts or difficulties be repurposed for God's Kingdom?
- What dividing walls of hostility is God asking you to help tear down?

Points for Prayer:

- For continued unity between former enemies now serving Christ together

- For healing of war-torn regions through the power of God's Word
- For courage to reach across ethnic and cultural divides with the Gospel
- For God to raise up more unlikely partnerships for Bible distribution

Prayer Response:

Prince of Peace, we stand in awe of Your power to transform enemies into brothers, soldiers into servants of Your Kingdom. Thank You for testimonies like Drasko and Jura's that remind us no divide is too deep for Your reconciling love. Help us see beyond our human divisions to embrace the unity You died to create. Use us, like these brothers, to build bridges where others see only walls. May our own unlikely friendships testify to Your power to heal history's deepest wounds.

Marina's Awakening:

From Confusion to Christ

---

2 0 2 0 s

"The unfolding of your words gives light; it
gives understanding to the simple."

PSALM 119:130

I N SMOLENSK, RUSSIA, where ancient streets have witnessed centuries of spiritual searching, God orchestrated a
story of transformation that began not in a church, but in the
depths of personal crisis. At twenty-eight, Marina stood at life's
crossroads, her path obscured by confusion and emptiness that no
earthly wisdom could illuminate.

Far from faith and religious tradition, she wandered through her days like a ship without anchor, her life at age twenty-eight becoming increasingly rudderless. Yet in this very emptiness, God was preparing soil for seeds of truth to take root. As one ministry partner would later reflect, "She was completely confused in life, which had become empty for her."

The divine appointment came through a simple invitation—a friend suggesting she attend a church service one Sunday. In that moment, what could have been just another declined invitation instead became a door into eternity. Marina stepped through, not knowing she was walking into her own transformation story.

What happened next bears the fingerprints of divine intervention. Someone offered her a Bible - not just any Bible, but one specifically provided through EEM's ministry. In those pages, Marina discovered not just words, but living truth that began to reshape her understanding of both God and herself.

Time passed, marked not by empty days but by deepening revelation. Marina later testified that this Bible had become her guide to understanding Christ, strengthening her newfound faith, and comprehending God as He truly is, rather than as she had imagined Him to be. Her transformation became a testament to the Holy Spirit's work through Scripture, proving that no life is too confused for divine clarity to penetrate.

What makes Marina's story particularly powerful is its reminder that God often works through the very emptiness we try to escape. Her confusion became the space where truth could echo, her searching the pathway to finding, her emptiness the vessel God chose to fill with His presence.

Questions for Reflection:

- Where might your own confusion or emptiness be preparing you for God's truth?

- How has Scripture transformed your understanding of both God and yourself?
- Who have you invited to church recently?

Points for Prayer:
- For those feeling lost and confused in life
- For courage to accept invitations to encounter God
- For Scripture to illuminate darkened understanding
- For those distributing Bibles to seekers
- For more lives to be transformed through God's Word

Prayer Response:
Lord of the Lost, we thank You for finding those who don't even know they're searching for You. Thank You for using emptiness as a gateway to fullness, confusion as a pathway to clarity. Help us recognize the divine appointments You arrange in ordinary moments, and give us courage to step through the doors You open. May we, like Marina, find in Your Word the truth that sets us free.

From War to Worship:

Constantine and Anastasia's Journey

2022

---

*"Come to me, all you who are weary and
burdened, and I will give you rest."*

MATTHEW 11:28

I
N THE BESIEGED city of Mariupol, Ukraine, where the
very air trembled with the thunder of war, God was writing a
story of salvation that would unfold like a flower in the midst
of rubble. Constantine, his wife Anastasia, and their two-month-
old son Timothy found themselves living a nightmare that would
transform into a testament of divine providence.

The rhythm of their days had become a desperate dance with

survival. While artillery fire painted the sky with death, they sheltered in their basement, venturing out only during brief respites to cook food in the open air. Constantine, carrying the weight of his community's grief, joined other men in the somber task of burying the dead in bomb craters twenty-two feet deep. In a city where normal commerce had collapsed, he witnessed the cruel mathematics of war – a car exchanged for a pack of cigarettes, fuel sold at impossible prices.

When their infant son Timothy developed dysbacteriosis, an imbalance in the composition and function of the gut's microbial community, Constantine faced a father's most haunting choice. Through streets where death waited in every shadow, he walked six miles to trade precious medicine for a pack of diapers. Each step was a prayer, each breath a reminder of their desperate need for divine protection.

The day before their district was to be "cleared," the young family gathered what little they could carry and fled on foot. Through a landscape transformed into a deadly maze, they darted from backyard to backyard, diving into craters at the whistle of incoming shells. Death seemed to wait around every corner, yet somehow they pressed on, their infant son clutched close, until a car appeared like manna from heaven to carry them to Zaporizhia, Ukraine.

But God wasn't finished with their story. At each stop along their refugee journey–Zaporizhia, Kamyanske, and Rivne, in Ukraine–they encountered something unexpected: Christ's church, arms open wide, meeting their physical needs while offering something more precious than bread. When offered a Bible, Constantine and Anastasia accepted it eagerly, memories stirring of childhood encounters with faith at Christian camps.

The transformation that followed defied human explanation. Constantine, after ensuring his wife and child's safety with relatives, made the decision to return to the edges of hell–not fleeing from Mariupol this time, but heading toward it to evacuate others. But he went as a different man. In Kamyanske, he had given his life to

Christ, downloading a Bible on his phone before departing. "I'm not afraid of death anymore," he declared to fellow believers, "since I'm one of you. I have to go there to rescue my family!"

In the crucible of war, where faith is stripped to its essence, Constantine and Anastasia's story reveals how God uses even the darkest circumstances to draw hearts to His light. Their journey from refugees to believers, from survivors to servants, testifies to the transformative power of encountering Christ in the midst of chaos.

Questions for Reflection:

- How does extreme hardship open our hearts to God's presence?
- What does Constantine's return to help others teach us about transformed faith?
- Where do we see God's protection in seemingly hopeless situations?

Points for Prayer:

- For refugees fleeing conflict zones
- For those returning to dangerous areas to help others
- For churches serving displaced people
- For protection over young families in war zones
- For continued transformation of lives through crisis

Prayer Response:

Lord of refuge, we stand in awe of how You work even through the darkness of war to draw hearts to Your light. Thank You for the testimony of Constantine and Anastasia, showing us that no circumstance is beyond Your redemptive touch. Protect those fleeing conflict today, strengthen those who return to help others, and continue to transform lives through Your Word even in earth's darkest valleys. May we, like Constantine, find courage to serve others once we've encountered Your saving grace.

The Nurse's Return:

A Divine Appointment in Lithuania

2020s

*'And we know that in all things God works
for the good of those who love him, who have
been called according to his purpose.'*

ROMANS 8:28

I N THE STERILE corridors of a Lithuanian intensive care
unit, where life and death wage their ancient battle, God was
orchestrating a reunion that would transform a medical crisis

into a miracle of faith. The story begins not with a conversion, but with a conversation—one that could only happen through divine timing and a mysterious illness.

A church leader in Klaipeda, Lithuania, found himself suddenly thrust into the realm between life and death, his body failing for reasons doctors struggled to understand. In the ICU, where machines beep out the rhythm of uncertainty, a nurse in full protective gear became his daily guardian angel. Through layers of PPE that obscured her face, she ministered to him with extraordinary care, becoming a vessel of God's healing touch.

Against all medical predictions, the man recovered completely. He returned to his weekly ministry of distributing Bibles on the streets of Klaipeda, sharing God's Word with any who would receive it. But God wasn't finished writing this story. Months later, during one of these street ministry sessions, he encountered a familiar face—the very nurse who had cared for him during his darkest hours.

She had been searching for him, drawn by an inexplicable need to know the outcome of his remarkable recovery. But God had prepared this moment for something far greater than a medical follow-up. As they spoke, the former patient became the minister, sharing not just the story of his physical healing but the greater story of spiritual healing available through Christ.

The nurse, moved by both the miracle she had witnessed and the testimony she now heard, found herself drawn to the very God who had used her hands in the healing process. The Bible she received that day became not just another book, but the beginning of her own journey of faith.

In this providential ordering, we see how God uses our deepest trials as preparation for ministry. A hospital room becomes holy ground; a medical crisis becomes a missionary moment; a chance reunion becomes a divine appointment. The leader's testimony of healing opened a door that no amount of street preaching could have unlocked.

Questions for Reflection:
- How might your current trials be preparing you for future ministry?
- When have you seen God orchestrate "chance" encounters for His purposes?
- What healing in your life could become a testimony to lead others to Christ?

Points for Prayer:
- For healthcare workers seeking spiritual truth
- For those currently in medical crisis
- For eyes to see divine appointments in daily encounters
- For courage to share our testimonies of healing
- For those who minister in streets and hospitals

Prayer Response:
Sovereign Lord, we marvel at Your ability to weave together the threads of our lives into tapestries of redemption. Thank You for turning our trials into testimonies and our suffering into opportunities for service. Help us recognize the divine appointments You arrange, and give us courage to share our stories of healing with those You bring across our path. May we, like this faithful leader, see every encounter as an opportunity to share Your love.

Tetyana's Awakening:
When Age Finds Truth

2022

> *"Even to your old age and gray hairs I am he,*
> *I am he who will sustain you. I have made you*
> *and I will carry you; I will sustain you*
> *and I will rescue you."*

ISAIAH 46:4

I N THE SHADOW of war's devastation, where age often becomes a burden too heavy to bear, God began writing a story of awakening through an eighty-two-year-old woman named Tetyana. Her journey to faith proves that divine timing knows no age limit, and that spiritual hunger can flourish even in the winter seasons of life.

Tetyana's story began on the eve of Russia's full-scale invasion of Ukraine, when an inexplicable spiritual burden drew her to church services. She came not alone, but with her son—a man with cerebral palsy who had been her constant companion through life's long journey. Together they formed an unlikely pair of seekers, their very presence a testament to perseverance.

As missiles began to fall and half their city fled into exile, Tetyana and her son remained behind, unable to navigate the chaos of evacuation. In their apartment, where the thunder of war became their daily soundtrack, something remarkable began to stir. The words she had heard in those few precious church services before the invasion took root in unexpected ways.

In the darkness of air raids, when others descended to basement shelters, Tetyana found herself offering what she called "clumsy prayers" – heartfelt conversations with a God she was just beginning to know. Unable to frequently seek shelter because of her son's condition, they remained exposed to danger. Yet in their vulnerability, they discovered a deeper protection—the presence of the One who watches over both young and old.

When the immediate threat subsided and she could return to church, Tetyana came not as a casual seeker but as one who had encountered God in the crucible of crisis. Her baptism, at eighty-two, became a powerful reminder that it's never too late to begin again in Christ. The Bible she received became not just another book, but a companion for the journey ahead.

In Tetyana's story, we witness how God's timing transcends our human understanding. Her journey reminds us that spiritual awakening can come at any age, that divine protection manifests in unexpected ways, and that sometimes the most profound faith emerges from what we might consider "clumsy prayers."

Questions for Reflection:

- How do we limit God's work by our assumptions about age?
- Where might God be using our "clumsy prayers" as bridges to deeper faith?
- What awakening might He be preparing in those we consider unlikely seekers?

Points for Prayer:

- For elderly seekers discovering faith late in life
- For caregivers carrying double burdens of physical and spiritual care
- For protection over vulnerable believers in war zones
- For churches ministering to older adults
- For those offering "clumsy prayers" to find God's heart

Prayer Response:

Father of All Ages, we thank You for Tetyana's testimony that reminds us Your grace has no age limit. Thank You for hearing our clumsy prayers and turning them into pathways of faith. Give us eyes to see the spiritual hunger in those we might overlook, and hearts to welcome seekers of every age into Your family. May we, like Tetyana, never consider ourselves too old for new beginnings in You.

Bible

Distribution

and Impact

The Bulgarian Revival:

How One Bible
Sparked a Movement

2018

"For the word of God is alive and active.
Sharper than any double-edged sword."

HEBREWS 4:12

I N THE FORGOTTEN corners of Eastern Europe, where
Soviet shadows once stretched long and dark, Bulgaria stood
as a testament to spiritual poverty in a post-communist world.
Often last on any list, this nation carried the weight of decades

under Soviet occupation, from 1944 until 1989, leaving a legacy of spiritual hunger that few eyes noticed and fewer hearts mourned.

When Dimitrios, EEM's Director for Southern Balkans, visited a small Bulgarian church, the scene that unfolded captured both the depth of need and the stirring of divine response. As he rose to preach and spoke those familiar words, "Turn in your Bibles to 1 Corinthians 13," what happened next pierced his heart. The entire congregation rose as one and moved toward the back of the room.

There, in a moment that would forever change his perspective on spiritual privilege, Dimitrios witnessed something extraordinary – the entire church gathering around a single Bible. They clustered together, peering over shoulders, stretching to see the precious words of the one Bible they had access to. None had copies at home; this solitary book was their only window into God's Word. So Dimitrios told them that when he returned again he would bring a Bible for each member of that congregation.

This scene, reminiscent of medieval times when Scripture was chained to pulpits, spoke volumes about the lingering effects of communist suppression. Yet in this picture of poverty lay the seeds of multiplication. God was already moving, turning scarcity into abundance through the distribution of over 100,000 Bibles and Bible-based books throughout Bulgaria in the following year.

When Dimitrios returned, the scene had transformed. Where once a single Bible drew a crowd, now multiple copies were available for eager hands. The image of that first visit–believers clustering around one precious book–had become a catalyst for change, a reminder that God's Word, like the loaves and fishes, multiplies in His hands to feed multitudes.

In this story of Bulgaria's spiritual awakening, we see the ancient truth that God's Word never returns void. Even in lands long forgotten by the world, His truth finds soil in hungry hearts, transforming spiritual poverty into abundance one Bible at a time.

Questions for Reflection:
- How do we value the access we have to God's Word?
- Where might God be calling us to notice and respond to spiritual poverty?
- What "single Bible" moments in our own lives have catalyzed greater multiplication?

Points for Prayer:
- For continued Bible distribution in spiritually impoverished regions
- For believers making do with limited access to Scripture
- For the multiplication of God's Word in forgotten places
- For hearts to remain hungry for truth despite scarcity
- For more eyes to be opened to the needs of overlooked nations

Prayer Response:
Lord of abundance and scarcity, we stand humbled by reminders of how precious Your Word truly is. Thank You for those who recognize and respond to spiritual hunger in forgotten places. Help us never take for granted our access to Your truth. Multiply Your Word in places where it remains rare and precious. May we, like those Bulgarian believers, hunger enough for Your truth to gather around even a single copy, trusting You to multiply our small provisions into feast for many.

The Thessaloniki
Encounter:

A Bible 12 Years in Waiting

2010s

"In their hearts humans plan
their course, but the Lord
establishes their steps."

PROVERBS 16:9

IN THE ANCIENT streets of Thessaloniki, Greece, where Paul once walked and preached, God was orchestrating a modern testimony through a simple misunderstanding. Sometimes divine appointments wear the disguise of interruptions, and heaven's purpose often hides behind human confusion.

The scene unfolded during the "Anastasi" Conference, its very name echoing resurrection hope. As believers took to the streets distributing Greek New Testaments, they carried not just books but seeds of transformation. Yet God's most profound work that day would spring from what appeared to be an interruption to their carefully laid plans.

A man stood working on his car, creating a moment of uncertainty for the Scripture bearers. They had been specifically instructed not to approach businesses, fearing potential police intervention. As Tamika Rybinski, EEM's graphic artist, passed by, she felt a divine nudge to offer this man a New Testament. This simple act of holy disobedience would open a door that no one expected.

As the team completed their rounds and retraced their steps, the same man beckoned them to return. Hearts tightened, expecting the confrontation they had been warned about. Instead, his face brightened with genuine wonder as he asked, "These New Testaments, they are Christian New Testaments, right?" Upon seeing the seal of approval from the Greek Orthodox Patriarch on the imprint page, his response pierced straight to the heart of divine purpose.

"I've lived in this neighborhood for twelve years," he shared, his voice carrying the weight of revelation. "We get offered books by Jehovah's Witnesses many times, but you are the first Christians to bring us the Bible in all these years!" His words laid bare both a tragedy and a triumph—twelve years without access to Scripture, yet God had preserved his hunger for authentic truth.

In this simple exchange, we glimpse how God often works through our holy uncertainties. What might have been dismissed as too risky became a divine appointment. A man's simple car repair became an opportunity for eternal maintenance. The very scenario workers had been warned against became the day's most powerful testimony.

Questions for Reflection:
- Where might our caution be preventing divine appointments?
- How does God use our uncertainties for His purposes?
- What "interruptions" in our lives might actually be divine invitations?

Points for Prayer:
- For discernment in recognizing divine appointments
- For courage to step beyond comfortable boundaries
- For those waiting years to receive authentic Scripture
- For more workers willing to risk holy disobedience
- For wisdom in distinguishing divine nudges from human impulses

Prayer Response:
Master of divine appointments, we marvel at how You orchestrate eternal moments through human uncertainty. Thank You for those willing to risk stepping beyond safe boundaries when Your Spirit prompts. Help us discern between human caution and holy hesitation, between comfortable boundaries and divine barriers. May we, like these faithful workers, learn to recognize Your invitations in what appears to be interruption. Use our uncertainties as gateways to Your purposes.

Opening Hearts
Through Education:

Ukraine's Ministry of Education Story

2015

*"Train up a child in the way he should go, and
when he is old he will not depart from it."*

PROVERBS 22:6

I N THE GRAND corridors of Ukraine's Ministry of Education,
where Soviet-era emblems still whispered of a godless past, an
unprecedented transformation was about to unfold. The year

was 2015 and Ukraine stood at a crossroads between its communist heritage and an uncertain future. Few could have predicted that a pragmatic political decision would become a gateway for God's Word to reach millions of children.

The story began with a pattern that caught newly-elected President Poroshenko's attention. Amidst the stack of reports on his desk, certain regions in the report from his minister of education stood out with remarkable consistency: higher test scores, fewer discipline problems, and improved student outcomes. When he summoned his Minister of Education to explain this phenomenon, the answer was both simple and revolutionary—these were the regions where Christian ethics and Bible teaching had been introduced into the public school curriculum.

Poroshenko, though not a believer himself, was a businessman at heart. "If that's what's working," he declared, "we need to make this offering across the entire nation." Yet in a country where the poverty line matched that of Uganda and Tanzania, resources for such an ambitious undertaking were nonexistent. The need was clear, but the means seemed impossible.

Enter a pivotal meeting in a building that still bore the physical marks of Ukraine's communist past. Here, where hammer and sickle emblems were embedded in the floor like fossils of a defunct ideology, armed guards stood watch as EEM representatives were ushered into the Minister of Education's office. The tension was palpable—decades of suspicion toward religious organizations didn't dissolve overnight.

For twenty minutes, through an interpreter, the Minister expressed gratitude for EEM's work in helping restore a biblical worldview to Ukraine's children. Then, switching seamlessly to perfect English, he asked the question that would change everything: "So, how can I help you?"

When EEM representatives explained the occasional resistance from regional officials, his response cut through generations of fear: "This is old KGB fear. They are afraid. They believe if they help you, they will lose their job. This will happen no more." With these words, he ordered an official letter declaring EEM as partners and friends, welcoming their books in every school across Ukraine.

The impact rippled outward like waves on still water. Within months, what began as a small initiative in select regions expanded into a national movement. By the time war broke out years later, three-fourths of Ukraine's public schools had received Bibles through this partnership. More importantly, EEM had established itself as an organization of integrity, known for delivering on promises and maintaining high standards in their work.

This transformation wasn't just about books in schools—it represented a profound healing of historical wounds. In the very buildings where religious expression had once been punished, children were now freely exploring faith. The same governmental structure that had once worked to eradicate belief in God was now actively partnering to restore it.

Questions for Reflection:

- How has God used secular authorities to advance His Kingdom in your experience?
- Where do you see opportunities to influence education with biblical truth?
- What "old fears" might be holding you back from bold action for God's Kingdom?

Points for Prayer:

- For continued open doors in education systems worldwide
- For protection of Christian education initiatives
- For wisdom for educators incorporating biblical truth
- For students receiving Bibles in schools
- For government officials to remain supportive of biblical education

Prayer Response:

Lord of all wisdom, we marvel at how You can use even pragmatic decisions by secular leaders to advance Your Kingdom. Thank You for opening doors that seemed forever sealed by ideology and fear. Give us wisdom to see and seize similar opportunities in our own spheres of influence. Help us be faithful stewards of the doors You open, maintaining integrity and delivering on our promises.

The Power of Partnership:

Hellenic Ministries and the Farsi Bible Project

2016

"Now to Him who is able to do exceedingly abundantly above all that we ask or think, according to the power that works in us."

EPHESIANS 3:20

I N THE AUTUMN of 2015, as waves of refugees sought sanctuary on Greek shores, a simple phone call set in motion a
cascade of divine provision that would impact thousands. The

request seemed modest enough at first: Farsi Bibles for refugees arriving in Greece. But God had plans that would stretch both faith and resources far beyond initial expectations.

Bart Rybinski, Vice President of EEM's European Operations, made an early morning call to his U.S. colleague at EEM, with urgency in every word. "We've got a request for 10,000 Farsi Bibles," he explained. The questions that followed were straightforward: Could they secure the translation? Yes. Would the quality meet their standards? Yes. Could they achieve the necessary price point? Yes. With each affirmative answer, the door opened wider to what would become one of EEM's most ambitious projects.

By January 2016, just two months later, that initial request had swelled to 110,000 Bibles and New Testaments. The numbers might have seemed daunting, but for those watching God's hand at work, it was simply confirmation that He was orchestrating something extraordinary. Among the ministries crying out for these Bibles was Hellenic Ministries, led by Jonathan Macris, a Greek national whose heart burned to serve the refugees flooding his nation.

For Hellenic Ministries, the cost of providing Bibles had become almost prohibitive. At $17.47 per Bible, their dream of placing God's Word in the hands of every seeking refugee seemed impossible. When Jonathan expressed his need for 60,000 Bibles and New Testaments, EEM's response was disarmingly simple: "Okay." The brevity of that answer left him skeptical—until the day his daughter's phone call changed everything.

"Dad," she said, her voice filled with bewilderment, "there's a delivery. It's pallets of boxes—so many they had to put them in your office. You can't even walk in there anymore." When Jonathan asked what was written on the boxes, her answer was simple: "Just three letters: EEM."

The magnitude of this provision—a $1.5 million value in Bibles—meant far more than just books delivered. It meant Hellenic

Ministries could redirect precious resources to meeting the immediate physical needs of refugees: food, clothing, shelter. It demonstrated how God's economy works when organizations focus on their unique strengths and work together in Kingdom partnership.

This collaboration exemplified a profound spiritual principle: when God's people unite in service, He multiplies their effectiveness far beyond what any could achieve alone. EEM couldn't do the frontline work that Hellenic Ministries excelled at, but they could provide the tools needed for spiritual transformation. Together, they created a pipeline of hope that met both physical and spiritual needs.

The impact rippled outward in countless personal stories of transformation—refugees discovering hope in their heart language, workers able to offer both bread and the Bread of Life, ministries finding their resources multiplied through partnership. In the midst of what many saw as a crisis, God was writing a story of provision that would touch generations.

Questions for Reflection:

- How has God used partnerships in your life to accomplish more than you could alone?
- Where might God be calling you to step out in faith despite seemingly impossible numbers?
- How do you see working differently than human economics?

Points for Prayer:

- For continued strong partnerships between Christian organizations
- For wisdom in stewardship of resources
- For refugee ministries worldwide
- For those distributing Bibles in crisis situations
- For more opportunities to provide Bibles in heart languages

Prayer Response:

Lord of infinite resources, we stand amazed at how You multiply our humble offerings for Your glory. Thank You for showing us that partnership in Your Kingdom transcends human limitations. Help us be faithful with what You've entrusted to us, always ready to say "yes" when You call us to seemingly impossible tasks. May we never limit what You can do through willing hearts working together.

Breaking Boundaries:

Slovenia's Interfaith Bible Mission

2010s

---

*"How good and pleasant it is when God's
people live together in unity!"*

PSALM 133:1

IN THE STORIED halls of Slovenia's governmental offices,
where centuries of religious tradition held sway, God was orchestrating a moment that would transcend typical denominational
boundaries. Through the humble efforts of Steve, an American missionary, and his local partners, a simple New Testament translation
was about to find its way into the hands of the nation's President.

The beauty of this moment lay not in its political significance, but in its testimony to how God often works through unlikely partnerships to accomplish His purposes. That a Protestant mission organization's Bible would be presented through Catholic channels to a secular leader spoke volumes about divine wisdom in bridging traditional divides.

This gesture, though seemingly simple, carried profound implications for a nation still finding its spiritual identity after years of communist influence. Each person involved–from the missionary to the Cardinal to the President–became part of a larger narrative about how God's Word transcends human-made boundaries of denomination and tradition.

The presentation itself became a living parable of unity, demonstrating how Kingdom purposes often require us to reach across traditional divisions. In a region where religious identity often creates barriers rather than bridges, this collaboration stood as a testament to how God's purposes unite hearts that human traditions might separate.

Through this story, we witness how divine wisdom often works not by confronting established systems, but by working through them for Kingdom purposes. Like Joseph in Pharaoh's court or Daniel in Babylon, God continues to position His truth in places of influence through unexpected channels.

Questions for Reflection:
- How might God be calling us to work across traditional boundaries?
- Where do we see opportunities for unity in our own divided contexts?
- What role can Scripture play in bridging denominational divides?

Points for Prayer:

- For continued openness to God's Word in government circles
- For more partnerships that transcend traditional divisions
- For wisdom in navigating institutional relationships
- For hearts to remain focused on Kingdom purposes beyond denomination
- For more opportunities to share Scripture in places of influence

Prayer Response:

Lord of all wisdom, we marvel at how You orchestrate collaborations that transcend human divisions. Thank You for showing us through this story how Your purposes often unite those whom tradition might separate. Give us wisdom to recognize and embrace opportunities for Kingdom partnerships, even in unexpected places. Help us see beyond our own traditions to Your larger purposes. May we, like these faithful servants, learn to work together for Your glory regardless of denominational boundaries.

Macedonia's Revival:

Building Sacred Bridges

▬

2020s

▬

*"Make every effort to keep the unity of the
Spirit through the bond of peace."*

EPHESIANS 4:3

I N THE HEART of the Balkan peninsula, where ancient stones
whisper tales of empires risen and fallen, God was orchestrating a story of unity that would transcend centuries of division.
Macedonia, a land where Orthodox Christianity and Islam have
long drawn lines of separation, was about to witness how divine
wisdom could transform traditional barriers into bridges of grace.

The journey began with a simple gift–one thousand Croatian Bibles for Macedonian children living in Croatia. Yet God, the master storyteller, was weaving a narrative far grander than this initial chapter suggested. When the Children's Bible was translated into modern Macedonian, what might have remained a small cultural exchange suddenly opened doors to divine possibility.

In the ornate office of Archbishop Stephan, where centuries of Orthodox tradition lined the walls, an extraordinary scene unfolded. The head of the Macedonian Orthodox Church, together with the dean of their Orthodox Faculty and the Church's main Secretary, gathered to consider something unprecedented–partnership with Protestant organizations to place God's Word in children's hands.

The Archbishop's response pierced straight to the heart of divine purpose: expressing profound gratitude "in the name of the Macedonian people" for this work of translation and distribution. In a nation where over ninety-five percent of ethnic Macedonians belong to the Orthodox Church, this opening of arms to Protestant partnership spoke volumes about how God's Spirit moves beyond traditional boundaries.

The timing proved divinely significant. In a country with over thirty percent Muslim population, where refugees from the Middle East regularly pass through on their way to Western Europe, this initiative carried potential far beyond its immediate scope. Each Bible distributed became not just a book but a seed of truth planted in soil long waiting for such nourishment.

Perhaps most remarkably, this collaboration marked the first partnership between EEM and a national Orthodox Church for the spiritual benefit of the children in this country. In these halls of ancient faith, where change often moves at glacial pace, God was writing a new chapter of cooperation that could transform an entire generation's understanding of His Word. The result being hundreds of thousands of children's Bibles have been and continue to be distributed in the Macedonian language.

Questions for Reflection:

- How does God work through unexpected partnerships to accomplish His purposes?
- Where might traditional boundaries be hindering God's work in our own contexts?
- What role does children's ministry play in bridging historical divisions?

Points for Prayer:

- For continued openness between Orthodox and Protestant believers
- For children receiving Bibles to be transformed by God's Word
- For wisdom in navigating cultural and religious sensitivities
- For more unprecedented partnerships in God's Kingdom
- For Macedonia's spiritual revival across all communities

Prayer Response:

Master of unlikely alliances, we stand in awe of how You weave together threads of faith that tradition had long kept separate. Thank You for leaders willing to see beyond historical divisions to eternal purposes. Guide this partnership between ancient and modern expressions of faith, that together they might reach a new generation with Your truth. Help us recognize and embrace unexpected collaborations You orchestrate in our own spheres. May we, like these Macedonian leaders, be willing to step beyond tradition when Your Spirit leads.

Samuel's Mission:

A Child's Passion for Sharing God's Word

2021

*"Don't let anyone look down on you because
you are young, but set an example."*

1 TIMOTHY 4:12

IN THE HEART of Poland, where adult skepticism often casts long shadows over matters of faith, God chose to kindle a flame through the pure enthusiasm of a child. Samuel's story reminds us how the Kingdom of heaven belongs to those who receive it like little children, his innocent passion for Scripture becoming a beacon of light in his community.

From the moment Samuel first opened the free EEM-supplied Children's Bible, something extraordinary ignited in his young heart. While many might skim through such pages with casual interest, Samuel dove deep into the waters of God's Word, reading it cover to cover not once, but nearly ten times. Each reading seemed to stoke the fire of his love for God, transforming knowledge into an irrepressible desire to share.

What followed was a testament to how God can use the smallest vessels for His greatest work. With the simplicity that only a child could muster, Samuel approached his parents with a divine vision – he wanted to give Children's Bibles to his classmates. No complex evangelistic strategy, no carefully crafted presentation, just the pure desire to share what had transformed his own heart.

His parents watched in wonder as their son distributed forty Bibles among his classmates and friends, each gift a seed planted in fertile young soil. The remaining ten Bibles became precious cargo in Samuel's eyes, his enthusiasm undiminished as he eagerly awaited more opportunities to share. In his childlike wisdom, he understood something many adults struggle to grasp – that God's Word is a gift too precious to keep to oneself.

In the words of Jesus, "Let your light shine before others, that they may see your good deeds and glorify your Father in heaven." Samuel embodied this command with a child's beautiful simplicity. His light wasn't dimmed by doubts or complicated by adult hesitations. It shone with the pure radiance of one who had discovered treasure and couldn't wait to share it with others.

Through Samuel's story, we glimpse how God often chooses the youngest among us to demonstrate the essence of His Kingdom. In a world where evangelism can become burdened with strategy and complexity, one boy's straightforward love for God's Word and eagerness to share it cuts through to the heart of what it means to be Christ's ambassador.

Questions for Reflection:

- What can we learn from Samuel's childlike enthusiasm for God's Word?
- How might our own approach to sharing faith be complicated by adult hesitations?
- Where has God placed us to be like Samuel in our own spheres of influence?

Points for Prayer:

- For children discovering God's Word for the first time
- For the seeds planted through Samuel's Bible distribution
- For parents nurturing their children's spiritual enthusiasm
- For more childlike faith in our own walk with God
- For the recipients of Samuel's Bibles to be transformed

Prayer Response:

Loving Father, we thank You for young hearts like Samuel's that remind us of the pure joy of knowing and sharing Your Word. Thank You for showing us again that Your Kingdom belongs to those who receive it like children. Help us rediscover that childlike enthusiasm for Your truth, unburdened by adult complications and hesitations. May we, like Samuel, find simple joy in sharing Your Word with others. Let his story inspire us to shine our light with similar pure intention, that others might see and glorify You.

Bibles in the Digital Age:
Mihai and Sebastian's Mission

▬▬

2020s

▬▬

*"Declare his glory among
the nations, his marvelous
deeds among all peoples."*

PSALM 96:3

I
N THE BUSTLING city of Timisoara, Romania, where
ancient church spires pierce the sky alongside modern office
buildings, God was writing a story of multiplication that began
with a single act of generosity. It started when Mihai, his heart burning with evangelical fervor, attempted to give a Bible to a friend. The

friend's disinterest might have discouraged many, but for Mihai, it became the seed of something greater.

Life has a way of preparing us for God's purposes through unexpected trials. When serious illness confined Mihai to a hospital bed, uncertainty clouding his future, he made a covenant with God: "If You heal me, I will serve You however You wish." God answered, and Mihai emerged from his hospital stay with not just restored health, but a renewed mission.

True to his promise, Mihai began giving Bibles to friends again. When another friend requested a Bible but Mihai couldn't afford one, he didn't hesitate—he took a second job simply to purchase that single Bible. It was this kind of dedication that caught Sebastian's attention when their paths crossed, igniting a partnership that would transform their corner of God's Kingdom.

Together, they embraced modern technology for ancient purposes, creating Facebook pages offering free Bibles. What began as a simple outreach exploded beyond their wildest dreams. Within two years, their ministry grew to 17,450 followers across two pages, resulting in the distribution of over 42,000 Bibles and Bible-based materials. Their reach extended far beyond Romania's borders, touching lives in Australia, Japan, Canada, and even Chicago.

Behind these numbers lie countless stories of transformation. A woman, frightened by the war in Ukraine, found answers to life's deepest questions in the pages of her newly received Bible. A disabled man, living in an abandoned, rat-infested building, wept when Sebastian's mother hand-delivered a Bible, saying, "No one has ever given me anything for free, especially not a Bible."

Each morning brings new requests—Mihai's phone regularly shows numerous unanswered voicemails before breakfast. Sebastian maintains a spreadsheet with thousands of rows, each representing a soul hungry for God's Word. Their car trunks have become mobile libraries, filled with carefully wrapped Bibles ready for mailing.

Questions for Reflection:
- How might God be calling us to use modern technology for Kingdom purposes?
- What promise have we made to God that needs renewed commitment?
- How can seemingly small acts of generosity multiply in God's hands?

Points for Prayer:
- For Mihai and Sebastian's continuing ministry
- For those receiving Bibles to be transformed by God's Word
- For wisdom in using technology to spread the Gospel
- For resources to meet the growing demand for Bibles
- For protection and provision for Bible distribution efforts

Prayer Response:
Lord of multiplication, we stand amazed at how You can take one person's faithful commitment and transform it into a movement touching thousands. Thank You for young leaders like Mihai and Sebastian who combine ancient truth with modern methods to reach hungry souls. Help us see how our own talents and technology can be used for Your Kingdom. Give us the courage to make and keep costly promises to You.

The Chocolate Bar Trade:

Revival in Romania

2020s

---

*"Blessed are those who hunger and thirst for
righteousness, for they will be filled."*

MATTHEW 5:6

I N THE GENTLE folds of Cluj, Romania, where ancient
streets whisper stories of faith both lost and found, God was
orchestrating a moment of divine simplicity through the most
ordinary of objects—a chocolate bar and a Bible. This story reminds
us how heaven often touches earth not in grand cathedrals, but on
humble front porches where hearts remain open to wonder.

Istvan, a faithful servant with eyes to see God's hand in life's simple moments, carefully prepared a food basket for a family in need. With pastoral intuition, he placed two treasures atop the other provisions—a large chocolate bar and a children's Bible. What followed would become a testament to how God often speaks most clearly through unscripted moments of childlike faith.

As Istvan presented the basket to the young couple on their front porch, their six-year-old son could barely contain his curiosity. Squeezing between his parents' legs, he pulled the basket down to eye level, his gaze falling upon those two carefully placed items—temporal sweetness and eternal truth side by side.

What happened next pierced straight to the heart of spiritual hunger in Romania. Without hesitation, bypassing even the temptation of chocolate, the boy grabbed the Bible and darted back into the house, his voice trailing behind him with pure excitement: "I'm going to read this right now!"

In that simple moment, Istvan witnessed something far greater than successful charity work. He saw in this child's response a picture of his nation's growing spiritual awakening—people eager to read God's Word for themselves, hearts hungry not just for physical sustenance but for eternal truth.

This boy's immediate attraction to Scripture became a living parable of Jesus's words about receiving the Kingdom like a child. In his unfiltered enthusiasm, we glimpse what genuine spiritual revival looks like—not necessarily in grand movements or massive gatherings, but in individual hearts racing toward truth with unbridled joy.

Questions for Reflection:

- What does this child's choice between chocolate and Scripture teach us about genuine spiritual hunger?
- How might we be overlooking simple opportunities to share God's Word in our daily acts of service?

- What can we learn from childlike enthusiasm for spiritual truth?

Points for Prayer:
- For spiritual revival in Romania
- For children encountering God's Word for the first time
- For wisdom in combining physical and spiritual ministry
- For more hearts hungry for Scripture
- For those distributing Bibles alongside humanitarian aid

Prayer Response:
Father of simple gifts, we thank You for moments that remind us how Your Word satisfies deeper hungers than any earthly pleasure. Thank You for children who show us what genuine spiritual appetite looks like. Kindle that same pure enthusiasm in our own hearts for Your truth. Help us recognize and create opportunities to share Your Word alongside our acts of service. May we, like this young boy, run eagerly toward Your truth with undistracted joy.

Vadim's Vision:

Overcoming Obstacles for Faith

———

2020s

———

"For we live by faith, not by sight."

2 CORINTHIANS 5:7

I N THE QUIET corners of ministry, where God's attention to detail often shines brightest, a seven-year-old boy named Vadim would teach us something profound about spiritual hunger and divine provision. His story reminds us how the Lord sees not just masses of humanity, but individual hearts with unique needs and desires.

Most children his age might have been content with simpler

versions of Scripture, but Vadim's circumstances demanded something different. Struggling with very poor eyesight, he might have become discouraged from engaging with God's Word altogether. Instead, his inquisitive nature led him to an unusual request—an EEM supplied large-print Bible, typically reserved for adults.

There was something beautifully compelling about this young soul who loved to work with his hands and delighted in Bible stories. Rather than letting his physical limitation become a barrier between him and God's Word, Vadim's determination led him to seek out exactly what he needed. His request for a large-print Bible wasn't just about reading—it was about independence, about engaging with God's truth on his own terms.

In this simple story lies a profound truth about how God meets us exactly where we are, with exactly what we need. The same Word that brings wisdom to the aged can bring delight to a child. The same truth that challenges scholars can capture the imagination of a seven-year-old. And sometimes, the format matters as much as the content when it comes to making God's Word accessible to all.

Vadim's story challenges our assumptions about how children engage with Scripture. His desire to read God's Word independently, despite physical challenges, reminds us that spiritual hunger knows no age limit. In his simple request, we see echoes of the Psalmist's declaration: "I rejoice in your word like one who discovers a great treasure."

Questions for Reflection:
- How do we sometimes overlook individual needs in our ministry approaches?
- What can Vadim's determination teach us about overcoming barriers to God's Word?
- Where might we need to be more creative in making Scripture accessible to others?

Points for Prayer:

- For children with special needs seeking to engage with God's Word
- For wisdom in meeting individual spiritual needs
- For more creative approaches to Bible distribution
- For young hearts developing hunger for Scripture
- For removal of barriers preventing access to God's Word

Prayer Response:

Gracious Father, we thank You for Your attention to individual needs, as demonstrated in Vadim's story. Thank You for reminding us that no barrier is too great when a heart hungers for Your truth. Help us see and respond to the unique ways people need to encounter Your Word. Give us wisdom to remove obstacles that might prevent others from accessing Scripture, and grant us creativity in meeting diverse needs. May we, like Vadim, pursue Your truth with determination regardless of circumstances.

Eastern Whispers:

Alexander's Kazakh Mission

2020s

'How beautiful are the feet of those who bring good news!'

ROMANS 10:15

IN THE VAST expanse of Eastern Kazakhstan, where ancient steppes meet modern restrictions, a quiet revolution of the heart unfolds through the patient work of one man. Alexander's story isn't one of dramatic confrontations or public victories, but rather of wisdom finding its way through the narrow spaces of legal constraint, like water seeping through rock.

The law stands firm: Bibles can only be distributed within

registered church walls. Yet God's Word, like the wind that sweeps across Kazakhstan's plains, refuses to be confined. Through Alexander's faithful stewardship, what began as careful compliance with restrictions has blossomed into a network of hope spanning the region.

His ministry moves like ripples across still water–gentle, yet ever-expanding. One Bible finds its way into hungry hands, and the story spreads in whispers and quiet conversations. "There's a man," they say, "who can help you find what you're seeking." Alexander has become known not by loud proclamation, but by persistent presence, his name passing from seeker to seeker like a treasured secret.

What makes this story remarkable isn't just the number of Bibles distributed, but the way God's Word creates its own pathways through the fabric of society. Within the strict boundaries of legal requirements, a tapestry of transformation emerges. Churches once isolated find connection, families discover hope, and communities experience renewal–all through the patient work of one man who understood that sometimes the most profound revolutions begin with a whisper.

In Alexander's hands, each Bible becomes more than paper and ink–it becomes a seed planted in fertile soil, waiting to burst forth with new life. His work reminds us that God's Kingdom often advances not through dramatic gestures, but through faithful presence and persistent love.

Questions for Reflection:

- How can you work creatively within restrictions to share God's Word?
- What networks or relationships has God given you to expand His Kingdom?
- How might your faithful persistence in small things lead to larger impact?

Points for Prayer:

- For protection and wisdom for believers working in restricted nations
- For creative solutions to Bible distribution challenges
- For the softening of government restrictions on religious freedom
- For more workers like Alexander to rise up in restricted areas
- For the safe delivery and impact of each Bible distributed

Prayer Response:

Sovereign Lord, we thank You for faithful servants like Alexander who find ways to share Your Word despite restrictions. Give wisdom to those working in challenging environments, showing them creative ways to advance Your Kingdom while respecting authorities. Thank You for demonstrating how persistent faithfulness in small things can lead to widespread impact. Help us to be both wise as serpents and innocent as doves as we seek to share Your truth with others. May Your Word continue to spread and bear fruit in even the most restricted places.

Faith in Crisis

and Conflict

A Warehouse of Hope:
God's Word in Kyiv's Darkness

2022

"Your word is a lamp to my feet and a light to my path."

PSALM 119:105

IN THE GATHERING twilight of Kyiv, Ukraine, where war's shadow stretched across a nation holding its breath, a young woman named Dasha stood amid towers of Bibles, her heart heavy with an impossible decision. The air raid siren's mournful cry pierced the evening air, but she couldn't leave—not yet. With Russian forces advancing and their warehouse just eight kilometers from Bucha, the fate of thousands of Bibles hung in the balance.

"We faced a choice that felt like Solomon's wisdom," Dasha tells me, her eyes revealing depths of resolve forged in crisis. "Evacuate our precious cargo to safety, or distribute everything immediately. We chose distribution—though at the time, we couldn't have foreseen how God would weave this decision into His greater tapestry."

What followed in those desperate early days of invasion would become a testament to how heaven's timing transcends human understanding. As missiles carved fiery arcs across Ukrainian skies, another movement was silently taking place—God's Word penetrating hearts suddenly laid bare by the brutal exposure of war.

"The hunger for Scripture tripled almost overnight," Dasha explains, her voice softening with wonder. "People who had never opened a Bible were suddenly reaching for it with desperate hands. When everything temporal is threatened, eternal words become the only solid ground."

In bomb shelters across the besieged nation, where darkness was broken only by emergency generators and flashlights, a profound scene began to unfold. Hours stretched into days as families huddled underground, their world reduced to concrete walls and uncertainty. Yet in this confinement, many discovered an unexpected liberation.

"A woman from Mariupol read her entire Bible in two weeks while sheltering from bombardment," Dasha shares, tears gathering in her eyes. "She told me, 'I've attended Orthodox services all my life, but in that basement, I met God personally for the first time. He was no longer distant—He was sitting beside me in the darkness.'"

The timing defies coincidence. Just days before the invasion began, Biblica had completed a new Ukrainian translation—modern, accurate, accessible. Paper supplies that normally would have been scarce were mysteriously available. Funding had arrived in full. Like manna before the wilderness journey, God had positioned every resource before the need became apparent.

"Looking back, we see His hand so clearly," Dasha reflects. "He was preparing the table before the storm even gathered."

Within hours of the invasion, while most organizations scrambled to establish humanitarian corridors, EEM's spiritual supply lines were already operational. The warehouse that could have become a casualty of war instead became a wellspring of hope. Each Bible distributed before the Russian advance represented another flame kindled against encroaching darkness.

As physical battles raged overhead, a quieter but no less significant awakening spread through underground shelters. Strangers who might never have spoken in peacetime now passed worn pages between them, finding common ground in ancient words. Children too young to understand war found comfort in Bible stories, their innocent faces illuminated by both flashlights and newfound faith.

"War creates a terrible clarity," Dasha observes. "Suddenly, people recognize what truly matters. Material possessions, status, ambitions—all these fall away. What remains is the hunger for something—Someone—who transcends the chaos."

The enemy's strategy of scattering Ukrainians across Europe backfired in ways only heaven could design. As millions fled westward, they carried not just personal belongings but the Word they had discovered in crisis. Ukrainian refugees became inadvertent missionaries, their dog-eared Bibles bearing witness across borders.

In a Vienna refugee center, I met Olena, her weathered Bible clutched like a treasure map. "This isn't just a book anymore," she told me, fingers tracing passages marked with dates that corresponded to bombardments. "These pages record my history with God—how I met Him in darkness, how He spoke when all other voices were silenced by air raid sirens. Every underlined verse is a moment when heaven touched my bunker."

As Dasha oversees continued distribution efforts, she reflects on the paradoxical flourishing of faith amid destruction. "People ask if Bible distribution decreased during the war. Actually, it tripled. While missiles were forcing people underground, God was drawing them toward heaven."

What the enemy intended for Ukraine's devastation, God transformed into pathways for revelation. In temporary shelters and displaced persons camps, in subway stations converted to bunkers and basements illuminated by candlelight, His Word found fertile soil in hearts stripped of everything but essential questions.

This miracle continues today—ordinary workers using ordinary tools for extraordinary purposes. Warehouse forklifts become instruments of divine provision. Delivery vans navigate dangerous checkpoints carrying cargo more powerful than any weapon. And through it all, the light continues to penetrate darkness, one open heart, one turned page at a time.

Questions for Reflection:

- How does our faith respond when darkness seems to prevail in our own lives?
- What "ordinary tools" might God be wanting to use for extraordinary purposes through us?
- Where do we see God's light penetrating seemingly hopeless situations around us?

Points for Prayer:

- For protection of Bible distribution efforts in conflict zones
- For wisdom and safety for workers like Dasha
- For the Word of God to bring hope in war-torn regions
- For creative solutions to logistical challenges
- For the light of Christ to pierce war's darkness

Prayer Response:

Lord of light and darkness, we marvel at Your ability to push back shadows through the faithful work of Your servants. Thank You for those who, like Dasha, refuse to let war's chaos silence Your Word. Strengthen all who risk their lives to distribute Scripture in dangerous places. Help us recognize how You can use even ordinary tools—generators and forklifts—as instruments of Your Kingdom. May we, like these faithful workers, persist in spreading Your light no matter what darkness surrounds us. Amen.

Faith in Belarus:

Bibles and Peace Amid Political Unrest

2020

"Blessed are the peacemakers, for they will be called children of God."

MATTHEW 5:9

I N THE TENSE streets of Minsk, where the air crackled with the electricity of political unrest, God was orchestrating a testimony of courage that would defy both fear and power. Against the backdrop of disputed elections and Europe's "last dictatorship," believers were about to demonstrate how divine truth stands firm even when earthly foundations shake.

The official narrative claimed Lukashenko had secured nearly eighty percent of the vote, extending his two-decade grip on power. But as citizens flooded the streets in protest of electoral fraud, a different kind of demonstration was taking shape—one carrying not political signs but Bibles marked with the golden cross on black covers.

In the midst of brutal crackdowns, where even random passersby faced violence from security forces, Christians organized a peace march that would stand in stark contrast to the chaos around them. Their weapons were not stones or angry slogans, but the Word of God held high—many carrying Bibles provided by EEM, each one a quiet declaration that truth transcends political power.

The cost of such witness proved steep. One family who was passing out Bibles in Belarus felt the weight of opposition personally. Authorities warned their son he was "protesting illegally" and threatened to take away all of the family's children—a chilling echo of similar threats faced by others in the movement. Yet like the early apostles who declared they must obey God rather than men, these believers continued their peaceful witness.

Perhaps most powerfully, this story captured how God's Word becomes both comfort and courage in times of persecution. One man in the protest, photographed holding his Bible, had already endured two imprisonments. The threat of losing his children hung over him like a sword, yet still he stood, his Bible a testament to truth that no earthly power can ultimately suppress.

In these moments of crisis, where earthly power showed its brutal face, God's people demonstrated a different kind of strength—one that conquers not through force but through faithful presence, not through violence but through vulnerable witness to truth.

Questions for Reflection:
- How does God's Word provide courage in times of persecution?
- Where do we see peaceful witness confronting worldly power?
- What price might we be called to pay for faithful testimony?

Points for Prayer:
- For believers facing persecution in Belarus
- For protection of families threatened for their faith
- For wisdom in bearing peaceful witness amid unrest
- For courage to hold fast to truth under pressure
- For God's Kingdom to advance through faithful testimony

Prayer Response:
Lord of all truth, we stand amazed at the courage You grant those who face persecution for Your name. Thank You for faithful witnesses who demonstrate that Your Word stands firm even when earthly powers rage. Protect those threatened for their testimony, strengthen those who face imprisonment or loss, and guide Your church in bearing peaceful witness amid societal storms. Help us recognize where we too might be called to stand firm, holding Your truth high despite the cost. May we, like these Belarusian believers, find in Your Word the courage to face whatever opposition comes.

Crossing Barriers:

God's Work in Divided Cyprus

────

2020s

────

"There is neither Jew nor Gentile,
slave nor free, for you are
all one in Christ Jesus."

GALATIANS 3:28

O N AN ISLAND where ancient stones still whisper tales
of Paul and Barnabas, where the gospel first found government welcome through Roman proconsul Sergius
Paulus, a new chapter of faith was quietly unfolding. Cyprus, an
island divided since 1974 by a UN buffer zone separating Greek

and Turkish populations, was about to witness how God's Word transcends human boundaries.

The story's historical weight rings with divine irony. This very soil, which first welcomed Christian administration in the world through Sergius Paulus's conversion, had become a testament to humanity's stubborn divisions. Since Turkey's invasion in response to a Greek-backed coup, the island had lived a fractured existence—Greek-speaking Cypriots to the south, Turkish Cypriots to the north, their separation marked by concrete walls, barbed wire, and watchtowers.

Yet in this landscape of inherited hostility, where "Christian faith" often meant little more than cultural tradition, God was stirring hearts to see beyond ancient wounds. Greek-speaking Christians, their own hearts transformed by divine love, approached EEM with an unprecedented request—Turkish Bibles for their neighbors across the buffer zone.

This request, the first of its kind, carried echoes of the early church's revolutionary understanding that in Christ, "there is neither Greek nor Jew." These believers, choosing to see their Turkish neighbors not as historical enemies but as souls precious to God, embodied the same boundary-breaking spirit that marked Christianity's earliest days on their island.

The beauty of this initiative lies not just in its crossing of physical boundaries, but in its challenge to deeper divisions of heart and history. In a place where ethnic tension had become normal, where Christianity often served more as a cultural identifier than a transformative faith, these believers dared to imagine a different story—one where the good news once again transcends all human barriers.

Their effort stands as a modern echo of that ancient moment when Sergius Paulus "became a believer, for he was astonished at the teaching about the Lord." Today, as Turkish Bibles make their way across the buffer zone, they carry the same astonishing message–that God's love knows no borders, that His Word belongs to all people.

Questions for Reflection:

- What "buffer zones" in our own communities need God's Word to cross?
- How might our cultural Christianity prevent us from seeing others as God sees them?
- Where are we called to be agents of reconciliation across divided spaces?

Points for Prayer:

- For continued openness to God's Word among Turkish Cypriots
- For believers taking risks to share across divisions
- For healing of historical wounds between communities
- For more initiatives that bridge ethnic and religious divides
- For Cyprus to experience renewal of its early Christian heritage

Prayer Response:

Lord of all peoples, we thank You for hearts brave enough to see beyond historical divisions to eternal possibilities. Thank You for this echo of Cyprus's first encounter with Your gospel, where once again Your Word crosses boundaries that humans cannot. Help us, like these Greek-speaking believers, to see our neighbors through Your eyes of love. May we, like Paul and Barnabas before us, be bold in sharing Your truth across every divide. Let Your Word once again astonish hearts on this historic island.

Sanctuaries in War:

Faith in Rivne's Bomb Shelters

▬

2022

▬

"God is our refuge and strength,
an ever-present help in trouble."

PSALM 46:1

I N THE BASEMENT sanctuaries of Rivne in Western Ukraine, where war's shadow threatened to extinguish all light, God was preparing spaces of extraordinary grace. As rumors of invasion gathered like storm clouds on the horizon, ministry partners moved with divine foresight, their hearts attuned to heaven's whispers of both warning and hope.

Just one week before war erupted across Ukraine's skies, these servants of God orchestrated what would prove to be prophetic preparation. Boxes of EEM Bibles made their way to partners in Western Ukraine, a movement of Scripture that would soon become a lifeline of hope for those fleeing eastward darkness. Heaven's timing displayed itself with devastating beauty—within days, the trickle of displaced souls would become a flood.

In the church basements that would become bomb shelters, God's servants created spaces that spoke to both body and soul. Alongside practical provisions—styrofoam for safety, humanitarian aid for survival—they placed tables laden with eternal treasure: Bibles for adults, coloring books filled with Scripture for children, literature that would transform into worship spaces.

These shelters became more than mere refuges from physical danger; they evolved into sanctuaries where young hearts could encounter divine hope. Children who might have been overwhelmed by the sounds of war above found themselves immersed in activities that spoke of peace beyond understanding. Each Bible coloring book story colored, each verse learned, became a thread of light woven through the fabric of their darkened world.

The prayer of those serving in these sacred spaces echoes with particularly poignant hope: "Lord! Bless the children of Ukraine to love you from their very childhood. May they learn God's Word and grow honest, just, and brave citizens of our country!" In these words, we hear the heart of those who see beyond present darkness to future dawn, who recognize that even in war's shadow, God prepares a generation for His purposes.

These basement sanctuaries stand as testament to how God often works most powerfully in our darkest spaces. In places meant for shelter from death, Life itself made its home. Where fear might have reigned, faith found fertile soil. What might have been mere waiting rooms became classrooms of grace, where young hearts learned that no darkness can overcome divine light.

Questions for Reflection:

- How does God use spaces of refuge for purposes of transformation?
- Where might He be calling us to prepare sanctuary for others?
- What role does preparation play in divine providence?

Points for Prayer:

- For children finding God's Word in places of refuge
- For wisdom in creating spaces of both physical and spiritual safety
- For those preparing sanctuaries in dark times
- For the next generation being shaped by crisis and faith
- For divine light to penetrate war's darkness

Prayer Response:

Father of Light, we marvel at Your ability to transform spaces of fear into sanctuaries of faith. Thank You for those who saw beyond immediate danger to eternal opportunity, preparing places where Your Word could reach searching hearts. Guide those creating spaces of refuge today, that they might tend to both body and soul. Help us recognize how You use even the darkest basements as classrooms of grace. May we, like these faithful servants, prepare well the spaces You entrust to us, knowing that every shelter can become sacred in Your hands.

Hope Among Ruins:

Ministry in Ukraine's War Zones

2022

*"For I was hungry and you gave me something to eat, I
was thirsty and you gave me something to drink."*

MATTHEW 25:35

IN THE HAUNTED spaces of war-torn Ukraine, where
air raid sirens replaced the gentle sounds of rural life, God
orchestrated stories of hope through the most unlikely circumstances. Through dedicated ministry partners working village by
village, divine grace flowed into places where the raw wounds of
war wrote their stories on every street corner.

The numbers tell their own story of divine provision - over

twenty-seven tons of humanitarian aid distributed, more than 14,000 miles traveled through dangerous territories. Yet behind these statistics lie countless personal encounters where physical provision opened doors for spiritual hope. In Kherson alone, the distribution of 1,500 fresh loaves of bread became more than sustenance; each piece became a symbol of hope, a reminder that even in war's wasteland, God still provides daily bread for His children.

Ministry workers moved with quiet determination through villages marked by warning signs declaring "MINED!" and past toppled electric poles standing like broken sentinels in empty fields. In their hands, food packages and winter supplies accompanied something even more precious—God's Word for those struggling with sickness and hopelessness.

The transformation wasn't just in those receiving aid. Workers themselves found their faith deepened by what they witnessed—how people who couldn't buy basic necessities for months would weep with joy at simple gifts, how those huddled in basements would gather to read Scripture together, how God's Word brought light to the darkest shelters. When gas supplies failed and homes grew cold, the delivery of 950 warm blankets became more than practical help; it became a tangible reminder that they were not forgotten by God or humanity.

In scenes reminiscent of early church accounts, these modern-day servants knelt to pray with the struggling, the sick, and the despairing. Their presence in each village became a living testimony that God had not abandoned these forgotten places. Every package delivered, every prayer offered, every Bible shared became a seed planted in soil watered by tears of sorrow and gratitude.

Through village after village, the pattern repeated—physical aid opening doors for spiritual comfort, practical help creating space for eternal hope. In places where war had stripped away every certainty, God's Word remained reliable and steadfast, bringing stability to shaken lives and hope to hearts heavy with fear.

This ministry of presence continues today, a testament to how God's light penetrates even the darkest valleys of human experience. Each delivery becomes more than mere humanitarian aid; it becomes a declaration that even in war's chaos, God's love finds ways to reach His children.

Questions for Reflection:

- How does God use times of crisis to reveal His presence in new ways?
- Where do you see opportunities to meet both physical and spiritual needs in your community?
- What role does consistent presence play in effective ministry during times of crisis?

Points for Prayer:

- For protection of aid workers in dangerous areas
- For wisdom in combining physical and spiritual ministry
- For hearts to remain open to God's Word amid suffering
- For continued provision of resources for humanitarian aid
- For peace in Ukraine's war-torn regions
- For those risking their lives to help others
- For creative solutions in reaching isolated communities

Prayer Response:

Master of divine provision, we stand in awe of how You weave hope through the fabric of despair. Thank You for servants willing to enter dangerous spaces carrying Your love. Guide those distributing aid in war-torn regions, protect those making perilous journeys to help others, and strengthen those who find ways to survive amid destruction. Help us see opportunities to be Your hands and feet in our broken spaces. May every piece of bread distributed, every blanket shared, and every Bible given become a testament to Your unfailing care.

Divine Choreography:

Guardians and Exodus
in Avdiivka

---

2 0 2 3

"When you pass through the waters, I will be
with you; and when you pass through the
rivers, they will not sweep over you."

ISAIAH 43:2

I N THE RAVAGED city of Avdiivka, Ukraine where time itself
seems measured by the rhythm of artillery fire, God writes
stories that defy human understanding. Among the 1,700 souls

who remain amid ruins that were once homes, heaven's timing intersects with earth's desperate needs in ways that transform both those who serve and those waiting for rescue.

For the Hands of Help team led by Oleksandr, ministry unfolds in impossible mathematics—brief six-minute windows before relocating to escape incoming shells. In these fleeting moments, eternal transactions take place: Bibles delivered, prayers offered, hope kindled in a landscape of despair. Their journey reads like a modern-day Acts of the Apostles, each dangerous street becoming holy ground where divine protection manifests in unexplainable ways.

Within this same fractured cityscape lived Lyudmyla and her son Dima, their story unfolding in trembling moments where a mother's love met heaven's provision. Standing in rooms that shook with each explosion, they found themselves at the crossroads of desperation and divine appointment, their tears mixing with the dust of constant bombardment.

What happened next reveals God's perfect choreography. During one of their ministry windows of opportunity, the team received word of Lyudmyla's situation. As they set out to reach her, artillery fire blocked their intended path. After prayer, something shifted in the spiritual atmosphere. Moving forward, they witnessed God's perfect timing as the shelling ceased long enough for their passage—only to resume behind them like the waters of the Red Sea closing after Israel's exodus.

The reunion with Lyudmyla and Dima became more than a rescue—it became a sacred intersection where ministry and exodus converged. Within hours, mother and son found themselves traveling toward safety with the very team that had come bearing Bibles and prayer. "We've grown to love them deeply," reflected one team member, "and they reciprocate that love. Beyond physical aid, we simply want to stand by them as they stand by us."

In the days that followed, God provided a new home for Lyudmyla and Dima near Kyiv, transforming their exodus into a journey of both physical and spiritual renewal. Yet their connection to the Hands of Help team endures, bound by sacred moments shared in Avdiivka's dangerous corridors.

What makes these converging stories particularly powerful is how they reveal God's ability to work through both those who stay to serve and those who must flee to survive. In a city where human wisdom says "Stay away," divine love says "Go deeper." Where human desperation cries "Help us escape," divine providence says "I have prepared the way."

Their intertwined testimonies ring with ancient truth—that God still parts waters and stills storms for His children, that divine timing transforms impossible situations, and that in places where destruction reigns, hearts unite in bonds that transcend circumstance.

Questions for Reflection:

- Where is God calling you to recognize divine timing in both staying and leaving difficult situations?
- How might your "impossible" circumstances become opportunities for ministry or deliverance?
- What "Red Sea" is God asking you to face with faith right now?

Points for Prayer:

- For protection over ministry teams serving in dangerous areas
- For wisdom in balancing courage with prudence
- For healing for traumatized families like Lyudmyla and Dima
- For the 1,700 souls remaining in Avdiivka

Prayer Response:

Lord of Perfect Timing, we stand in awe of Your choreography in places where human hope seems shattered. Give courage to those facing their own Red Sea, wisdom to those You send as deliverers, and love that compels us beyond our fears. May we learn to move in step with Your perfect timing, finding holy ground in the spaces between danger and divine protection. Amen.

Klavdiya's Twelve Days:

When Angels Feed Goats

2023

'Even when I walk through the darkest valley,
I will not be afraid, for you are with me.'

PSALM 23:4

IN THE PRE-DAWN darkness of June 6, 2023, when the Kakhovka Dam was breached and the waters of the Dnipro River surged without warning through sleeping villages below, God was preparing to write a story that would challenge the boundaries between miracle and mundane. As the floodwaters swept through Kohanivka and surrounding settlements, what would emerge was a testament to divine provision in humanity's darkest hours.

The destruction was catastrophic. The dam's breach sent a wall of water through countless communities along the Dnipro River in the Kherson Oblast, leaving a trail of devastation that would forever alter the landscape. Homes vanished beneath the muddy deluge, families were scattered, and entire villages disappeared under the rising waters. Many lost their lives; countless more lost everything they owned. The region would never be the same.

Yet in this landscape of loss, one story would emerge that testified to God's intimate care even in the midst of widespread devastation. It began not with thunder or proclamation, but with an elderly woman named Klavdiya Ivanivna, three unlikely animal companions, and a tiny wooden platform that would become their ark of survival.

As the waters rose with terrifying speed, Klavdiya found herself trapped, guiding her peculiar family—a goat, a dog, and a rooster—up a precarious ladder to her attic. In what could only be a Heavenly arrangement, she managed to shepherd all three animals to safety before the rising waters claimed her house key, dropping it into the muddy deluge below.

Their sanctuary measured no more than three feet square, a wooden platform near the attic doors that would become their home for twelve long days. In the mathematics of survival, this shouldn't have worked—four living creatures sharing a space barely big enough for one, with no food and no way to summon help. But God has always excelled at impossible equations.

As if orchestrated by unseen hands, a sack of grain somehow floated to their precarious perch - a provision so unlikely it could only be seen as divine intervention. This floating feast became their manna, sustaining both human and animal alike. The goat ate the grain and produced milk, which sustained both Klavdiya and her faithful dog. In this miniature ecosystem of survival, each creature played its part in a story of divine provision.

For twelve days, while snipers patrolled nearby and the waters raged below, this improbable family survived on their tiny platform. Their story became a living parable of God's provision—how He can multiply resources, create sustenance from scarcity, and preserve life in the most unlikely circumstances, even in the midst of man-made catastrophe.

When rescue finally came in the form of a local believer named Oleksandr, he found more than survivors - he found witnesses to a modern-day miracle. Their twelve-day vigil had become a testament to how God provides, not just in the grand moments of deliverance, but in the daily bread of survival, even when that survival seems mathematically impossible.

Today, Klavdiya's story echoes the biblical accounts of God's provision—the ravens feeding Elijah, the widow's oil that never ran dry. It reminds us that divine care often comes packaged in ways we least expect, through means we might never have imagined. A floating sack of grain becomes manna; a goat becomes a provider; a tiny platform becomes holy ground. Even amid historical catastrophe that would forever change the landscape of Kherson Oblast, God's provision proves greater than any human-made disaster.

Questions for Reflection:

- Where have you seen God provide in unexpected ways during your darkest times?
- How might your current limitations become platforms for experiencing God's provision?
- What "impossible equations" are you facing that require divine intervention?

Points for Prayer:
- For those currently trapped in seemingly impossible situations
- For eyes to see God's provision in unexpected places
- For faith to trust God's care even in confined spaces
- For those providing rescue and aid in disaster zones
- For multiplication of resources in times of scarcity

Prayer Response:
Provider God, we stand amazed at Your ability to sustain life in the most unlikely circumstances. Thank You for reminding us through Klavdiya's story that You can create abundance even in the smallest spaces. Help us trust Your provision when logic says survival is impossible. May we, like Klavdiya, become witnesses to Your miraculous care in the midst of life's floods. Give us faith to see beyond our limitations to Your limitless ability to provide.

Morning Star's Vigil:
The Watchmen of Vinnytsia

2023

'The people walking in darkness have seen a great light; on those living in the land of deep darkness a light has dawned.'

ISAIAH 9:2

IN VINNYTSIA, UKRAINE, where war has rewritten the rhythms of daily life, a church called Morning Star lives up to its celestial namesake, piercing the darkness with divine light. Their story unfolds not in grand gestures, but in the faithful presence of those who have taken up the ancient calling of watchmen on the walls.

Between October and November of 2023 alone, they ministered to 1,605 souls—314 men, 845 women, and 446 children. But these aren't merely statistics; they represent lives touched by hands that have learned to serve like Christ in the midst of chaos. Each number carries a story, a face, a name known to God.

In the heart of their ministry stands a unique space called "Workshop of Kindness," where children forced from their homes by war find moments of sacred normalcy. Here, amid art supplies and gentle guidance, 530 families have discovered that creativity can become a form of healing, that beauty can emerge from brokenness.

Their watchman ministry extends beyond city walls to villages where the war's impact lingers in destroyed homes and scarce resources. Every two to three weeks, they venture into frontline areas, carrying not just humanitarian aid but hope itself. When flooding destroyed vegetable crops and winter's chill threatened those in partially destroyed homes, Morning Star became God's hands, providing firewood, food, and shelter.

One church leader shared, "Together, we are approaching victory!" But the victory they speak of transcends military outcomes. It's the victory of light over darkness, of hope over despair, of faithful presence over fear. Their persistence in returning to dangerous areas speaks of a love that refuses to abandon those in need.

Questions for Reflection:
- Where has God called you to be a watchman in your community?
- How might creativity and kindness become instruments of healing?
- What does faithful presence look like in your context?

Points for Prayer:
- For protection of those serving in frontline areas

- For continued provision of resources for humanitarian aid
- For healing through creative ministries
- For strength for the watchmen who keep vigil
- For wisdom in meeting both physical and spiritual needs

Prayer Response:

Bright Morning Star, we thank You for those who stand watch in dark places, holding forth Your light. Bless the faithful servants in Vinnytsia who refuse to let war's shadow extinguish hope. Give them wisdom as they create spaces of beauty amid destruction, strength as they carry aid to dangerous places, and joy as they witness Your victory over darkness. May their example inspire us to be watchmen wherever You place us.

Ashes to Hope:

Hidden Treasures in Ukraine's Villages

2023

"The Lord is close to the
brokenhearted and saves those
who are crushed in spirit.

PSALM 34:18

I N THE GENTLE warmth of a Polish summer, where the trauma of war met the tender embrace of God's people, a remarkable story of transformation was unfolding. Members of the Zaporozhye, Ukraine church, themselves displaced into Poland by war, joined hands with American youth missionaries to create something unprecedented—a sanctuary of hope for fellow refugees seeking both shelter and spiritual solace.

For six precious days, the air rang with sounds that defied the nearby echoes of war—children's laughter mingling with prayer, songs of worship rising above the weight of displacement. Eighty children and forty adults, now all far from their Ukrainian homes, found themselves wrapped in a community that understood their journey intimately. These weren't just refugees serving refugees; they were witnesses to how God weaves new family tapestries from threads of shared suffering.

The path to this gathering began in the crucible of crisis, where the distribution of humanitarian aid had opened doors to deeper connections. What started as meetings of physical necessity had blossomed into spiritual kinship. The church had maintained these precious relationships throughout the year, understanding that ministry to displaced people requires not just initial aid but ongoing presence.

This wasn't merely a summer camp; it was a living testimony to how God transforms the story of displacement into one of divine appointment. Children who had known only the language of loss were now learning the dialect of hope. Parents who had carried the weight of uncertainty found shoulders to share their burdens. Together, they played, prayed, and studied God's Word, creating memories that would anchor their faith through whatever storms lay ahead.

The significance of this gathering extended beyond its immediate impact. Never before had a church in Poland attempted such a large-scale event for refugees. Its very existence testified to the power of partnership—local believers, American teams, and Ukrainian refugees coming together to create something beautiful from the ashes of war.

Through the generous support of partners, these families received more than just physical sanctuary Each one left with EEM Bibles, coloring books, and other Christian materials—seeds of truth to nurture the tender shoots of faith sprouting in displaced soil. In their hands, these weren't just books; they were anchors of hope, reminding them that even in exile, God's Word remains a constant companion.

Questions for Reflection:

- How does God use our own displacement to minister to others?
- What role does ongoing presence play in refugee ministry?
- How can we create communities of hope in the midst of crisis?

Points for Prayer:

- For displaced families finding community in exile
- For churches serving refugee populations
- For the children processing trauma through faith
- For continued provision of resources and support
- For more initiatives bringing hope to displaced people

Prayer Response:

Father of the displaced, we thank You for Your ability to create family from fragments, hope from heartache. Thank You for servants who see beyond immediate needs to eternal opportunities. Bless every seed of truth planted in young hearts at this camp. Strengthen those who minister to refugees, and help us all recognize how You can use our own experiences of displacement for Your glory. May we, like the Zaporozhye church members, learn to serve others even in our own season of need.

The Porto Astro
Awakening:

God's Movement Among Refugees

2023

'For I know the plans I have for you,' declares the
LORD, 'plans to prosper you and not to harm
you, plans to give you hope and a future.'

JEREMIAH 29:11

AGAINST THE SHIMMERING backdrop of Greek waters of the Aegean Sea, where ancient mariners once sought safe harbor, God has created a haven of hope at the Porto

Astro camp. Here, in a place where the rhythms of waves meet the rhythms of grace, nearly one hundred Ukrainian refugees discovered that displacement can become holy ground.

The story unfolds, not in the language of statistics, but in the quiet testimonies of transformed lives. Like Olya, whose journey began in the crucible of physical suffering. "I had lost hope," she confessed, her words carrying the weight of countless others who fled war's devastation. "But here, in this unexpected place, I truly found God." Even facing surgery, her testimony rings with profound peace: "I'm no longer afraid. My heart overflows with tranquility because I know He will sustain me."

August 2023 marked a divine appointment as the facility welcomed its displaced guests. But God was preparing something far beyond physical shelter. In the shared meals, in the late-night conversations, in the tears and laughter of the community, something profound began to stir. The Holy Spirit moved like a gentle Mediterranean breeze through broken hearts, awakening faith in souls who had lost everything but found Christ.

By summer's end, five people had walked into the baptismal waters, their stories becoming part of a larger narrative of redemption. Each baptism represented not just an individual decision, but a testament to how God transforms the pain of displacement into the joy of spiritual homecoming. Their emergence from the waters declared that even in exile, one can find ultimate belonging in Christ.

What makes the Porto Astro miracle particularly profound is how it demonstrates God's ability to create sacred space in the midst of crisis. Here, where the wounds of war meet the waters of baptism, refugees discover they are not just fleeing from something but being drawn to Someone. Their physical journey becomes a metaphor for a deeper spiritual pilgrimage.

Questions for Reflection:

- Where do you see God creating sacred spaces in unlikely places?
- How might your own experiences of displacement become pathways to ministry?
- What does it mean to find "home" in Christ when earthly homes are lost?

Points for Prayer:

- For continued spiritual awakening among refugees
- For healing of trauma through Christ's love
- For provision for the Porto Astro's Hellenic Ministry facility
- For wisdom for those ministering to displaced people
- For more baptisms and spiritual births among refugees

Prayer Response:

Lord of the Displaced, we thank You for turning Porto Astro into a sanctuary of hope. Thank You for showing us that no crisis is beyond Your redemptive touch, no journey too far for Your grace to reach. Help us see the sacred possibilities in every situation of displacement, and give us hearts to welcome those seeking both physical and spiritual refuge. May we, like those at Porto Astro, become witnesses to Your power to create home in the midst of exile.

Six Kilometers from War:

The Miracle of Siversk

2023

"So do not fear, for I am with you;
do not be dismayed, for I am your God.
I will strengthen you and help you;
I will uphold you with my
righteous right hand."

ISAIAH 41:10

I N THE WAR-TORN landscape of eastern Ukraine, where the mathematics of survival are measured in meters from the front line, God is writing a story of defiance against darkness. Siversk stands just six kilometers from where artillery fire punctuates each day's uncertainty, a city whose population has dwindled from 11,000 to 900 souls. Yet here, in this razor-thin margin between war and peace, divine light refuses to be extinguished.

The city bears the wounds of conflict openly—buildings scarred by shellfire, streets empty save for the occasional hurried figure, the constant background chorus of warfare. But in this unlikely soil, faith takes root with stubborn persistence. Those who remain are not just survivors; they become witnesses to how God's Word flourishes even in the valley of shadow.

Ministry teams move through the city like modern-day prophets, carrying not just humanitarian aid but something far more precious—the bread of life itself. Their movements follow a deadly choreography: a quarter-hour at most in any single location before retreating to safer ground. Yet in these narrow passages of time, eternal transactions take place.

"People do not have confidence in the next minute of life," one worker whispers, his eyes reflecting both sorrow and hope. "But faith in God and reading His Word help them to hold on and survive." The Bibles they distribute become more than books—they transform into anchors for souls adrift in war's chaos, compasses pointing toward hope when all other directions lead to despair.

In basements where residents huddle during shelling, these sacred pages become carriers of light in both literal and spiritual darkness. Stories emerge of elderly believers sharing Scripture with neighbors, of young mothers finding comfort in ancient promises, of faith taking root in soil saturated with suffering.

What makes the Siversk story remarkable isn't just survival against odds—it's the flowering of faith in circumstances designed to destroy it. Each Bible delivered becomes a declaration that God's Word cannot be silenced by artillery fire, that His truth penetrates even the darkest corners of human conflict.

Questions for Reflection:

- Where do you see God's light penetrating seemingly hopeless situations?
- How might your own valley of shadow become holy ground for ministry?
- What does it mean to be a carrier of God's Word into dark places?

Points for Prayer:

- For protection over the remaining residents of Siversk
- For wisdom and safety for ministry teams
- For the Word of God to take root in war-torn hearts
- For peace to prevail in Ukraine
- For those choosing to stay and minister in dangerous places

Prayer Response:

Lord of the Front Lines, we stand in awe of Your presence in places where human hope seems extinguished. Thank You for the testimony of Siversk, where Your Word proves stronger than warfare, Your light brighter than darkness. Strengthen those who carry Your truth into dangerous places, and help us remember that no circumstance lies beyond Your reach. May we, like these faithful few, become bearers of Your light in the darkest valleys.

Hope in Kramatorsk:
When Bombs Build Faith

2023

"For God, who said, 'Let light shine out of darkness,' made his light shine in our hearts to give us the light of the knowledge of God's glory displayed in the face of Christ."

2 CORINTHIANS 4:6

I N KRAMATORSK, UKRAINE, where air raid sirens have become a grim lullaby and buildings tremble beneath artillery's thunder, God weaves a story of defiance against despair. Here, on the razor's edge of war's fury, an unlikely hunger grows—not for bread alone, but for the eternal Word that feeds the soul.

The revelation comes from those serving on the frontlines of faith: "The large print Bible is very popular now," a ministry partner shares, voice thick with wonder. "For older people with poor eyesight, this is a balm." In a place where darkness threatens both physically and spiritually, God ensures His Word remains accessible to all who seek it.

Picture an elderly woman, her weathered hands trembling not from fear but from joy, as she receives a Bible with text large enough for her failing eyes to read. She nearly dances with delight, this unexpected gift becoming a light in her personal darkness. In a city where electricity flickers and fails, where internet connections dissolve into static, these printed words become more precious than gold.

The hunger for Scripture manifests in surprising ways. Those serving in Kramatorsk must navigate between bomb shelters and broken buildings, delivering Bibles alongside basic necessities. Each delivery becomes a sacred mission, every Bible a seed of hope planted in soil churned by conflict.

What makes this story particularly profound is how it challenges our understanding of spiritual awakening. Here, where every day brings new threats, where survival itself seems miraculous, people aren't turning away from faith - they're running toward it. The very conditions meant to break the human spirit instead kindle an unquenchable yearning for God's truth.

Questions for Reflection:

- How does physical darkness make us more aware of our need for spiritual light?
- Where do you see God making His Word accessible in unexpected ways?
- What role might your own trials play in deepening spiritual hunger?

Points for Prayer:

- For protection over Bible distribution efforts in war zones
- For those reading Scripture in bomb shelters
- For the elderly finding comfort in God's Word
- For wisdom in meeting both physical and spiritual needs
- For peace to prevail in Kramatorsk

Prayer Response:

Prince of Peace, we thank You for turning places of darkness into sanctuaries of light. We marvel at how You use even war's devastation to awaken spiritual hunger. Strengthen those who risk everything to deliver Your Word, and comfort those who find solace in its pages. Help us remember that no darkness - whether of war, aging, or despair—can overcome Your light.

Reaching
the Margins:
Ministry Among
the Overlooked

Ana's Love:

A Shelter for Croatia's Forgotten Children

2010s

"Religion that God our Father accepts as pure and faultless is this: to look after orphans and widows in their distress."

JAMES 1:27

IN THE QUIET corners of Zagreb, Croatia, where society's forgotten little ones find temporary shelter, God was writing a story of love through the dedicated heart of a house mother named Ana. When EEM provided her shelter with Children's

Bibles, she discovered they would become instruments of healing for wounded young souls.

The scene unfolds in a children's home where Ana serves not just as caregiver but as a vessel of grace to children who have known more of life's shadows than its light. Each day brings new challenges—emotional outbursts, desperate needs, hearts scarred by abandonment. Yet in this landscape of broken trust, Ana moves with a love that seems to draw from an endless well.

One particular day illustrated the extraordinary nature of this calling. A child who had experienced severe trauma was having an especially difficult time, emotions spilling over in ways that would test any caregiver's patience. As others stepped back, Ana stepped forward, wrapping arms of unconditional acceptance around the storm of pain. In her hands, she held an EEM Children's Bible, its pages filled with stories of a Father who never abandons His children. In that moment, something profound shifted—not just in the child, but in all who witnessed this display of love that transcends human logic.

"These children need more than just care," Ana would later share, her eyes reflecting both the weight and wonder of her calling. "They need to know they are worth loving, even when their behavior suggests they don't believe it themselves. These Children's Bibles help me show them a love bigger than their pain." Her words echo the very heart of divine love—how it pursues us not because we deserve it, but because love itself transforms us.

The impact ripples far beyond individual moments of crisis. Children who arrive believing they are unlovable gradually begin to glimpse their true worth through both Ana's consistent reflection of God's heart and the stories they discover in their Bibles. Each small victory—a trust slowly built, a Scripture passage understood, a hurt carefully healed—becomes a testament to how divine love works through both human hands and holy words to restore broken spirits.

When asked about what sustains her in this challenging ministry, Ana's response cuts straight to the heart of gospel truth: "Every time I reach out to one of these precious ones with God's Word and love, I remember how He reached out to me when I was far from lovable. How can I do less for these little ones He loves so dearly?"

Questions for Reflection:

- Where do we see God's unconditional love reflected in our own lives?
- How might we be called to demonstrate divine love in seemingly impossible situations?
- What role does consistent presence play in healing broken trust?

Points for Prayer:

- For house parents serving in children's homes
- For healing of traumatized children
- For wisdom in showing unconditional love
- For strength to maintain loving presence in difficult moments
- For more workers called to serve society's forgotten ones

Prayer Response:

Father of the fatherless, we stand in awe of how You channel Your love through willing vessels like Ana. Thank You for those who demonstrate Your heart by loving beyond logic and caring past convenience. Strengthen all who serve in children's homes, grant them wisdom in moments of crisis and endurance for the long journey of healing. Help us recognize opportunities to reflect Your unconditional love in our own spheres. May we, like Ana, become living testimonies to how Your love transforms both giver and receiver.

Toncka's Courage:

Love in Forgotten Roma Villages

2010s

"Perfect love drives out fear."

1 JOHN 4:18

I N THE SHADOWS of Slovenian society around 2018-2019, where Roma communities exist in the margins of acceptance, God was writing a story of courage through one woman's faithful heart. While others saw danger and chaos in Roma villages, Toncka saw children waiting to discover their heavenly Father's love. Her story reveals how divine purposes often unfold not in the spotlight of public acclaim, but in the quiet corners where most fear to tread.

The church's initial assessment seemed prudent enough—Roma neighborhoods were deemed too dangerous for outreach. Violence and chaos marked these communities as no-go zones, leading church leaders to reluctantly withdraw for their members' safety. But in that moment of collective retreat, one heart heard a different calling. Toncka, carrying nothing but faith and children's Bible lessons, stepped forward when others stepped back.

What began as one woman's solitary journey soon blossomed into something more. After those first tentative visits, Toncka brought a friend, and together they discovered something remarkable—their presence, focused solely on teaching children about God's love, was welcomed rather than rejected. Their reputation grew not through force or strategy, but through the simple power of showing up with God's Word and genuine care.

The transformation was profound. Villages once considered too dangerous for church outreach became fields of spiritual harvest. Toncka's courage opened doors that fear had kept firmly shut, and several churches began following in her footsteps, entering these communities with new eyes of faith rather than fear.

When resources for teaching seemed scarce, Toncka and church leaders prayed for God's provision. The answer came in 2018 with the first publication of Slovenian Coloring books from EEM, materials that Toncka described as gifts from heaven itself. These resources became bridges of understanding, allowing God's Word to cross cultural and linguistic barriers through the universal language of childhood wonder.

Perhaps the most beautiful fruit of this ministry emerged in the story of two Roma sisters who received Teen and Children's Bibles. These young girls, their hearts touched by God's Word, began teaching their father Marjan to read using the very EEM-supplied Bibles they had received. In this touching reversal, children became teachers, and Scripture became the key not just to spiritual literacy but to basic reading skills that had long seemed out of reach.

Questions for Reflection:

- Where might God be calling us to step forward when others step back?
- How can our simple acts of faithful presence open doors for broader ministry?
- What "dangerous" territories in our own communities need someone willing to enter with God's love?

Points for Prayer:

- For protection and wisdom for those ministering in challenging communities
- For Roma children and families discovering God's Word
- For more workers willing to enter difficult mission fields
- For transformation of communities through children's ministry
- For breaking down of prejudices and fears that hinder outreach

Prayer Response:

Lord of the margins, we thank You for servants like Toncka who demonstrate how Your perfect love casts out fear. Thank You for showing us again that Your Kingdom advances not through might or power, but through humble courage and faithful presence. Help us see beyond surface dangers to the hearts hungering for Your Word. Give us wisdom to know when to step forward in faith, even as others step back. May we, like Toncka, become bridges of Your love to those our society often overlooks.

Mahdi's Journey:

Grace in an Afghan Refugee's Life

▬▬▬

2010s

▬▬▬

"For the Son of Man came to seek and to save the lost."

LUKE 19:10

IN THE FLUID landscape of refugee ministry in Greece, where lives intersect like threads in an ever-changing tapestry, God was weaving a story of transformation through the quiet presence of a young Afghan photographer. Mahdi, age 25, moved through the chaos of refugee life with a reserved dignity, his camera capturing beauty in the midst of displacement while his heart secretly yearned for something his lens couldn't frame.

His role as a translator for a twenty-four-year-old journalism student, who was investigating the stories of her displaced contemporaries and researching Afghan refugees, seemed ordinary enough. Yet, even in this professional relationship, Mahdi's mature and gentle spirit became evident as he demonstrated respect for the younger journalist.

Through his photographer's eye, Mahdi captured the stunning vistas of his new Greek home, each image a testament to finding beauty in exile. But God was preparing to show him a different kind of beauty—one that no camera could capture. At a Monday night gathering where Muslim refugees received both physical and spiritual nourishment, Mahdi's journey toward faith began taking shape.

The stirring in his spirit started subtly, like a whisper in a storm, as he listened to others speak about Jesus and read from the Bible. "God was telling him that Jesus was his son," he would later explain, "and that he needed to follow him and make him and his teachings lord of his life." Yet this first stirring faded, leaving him in that liminal space between seeking and finding.

But God wasn't finished. As Mahdi observed the consistent love demonstrated by ministry teams and local believers, a profound realization began to dawn. "As I have watched your team," he shared, "you all are the same as the people from Hellenic Ministries and you all follow Jesus. I now know that it is real. Jesus is changing people, no matter where you are from, into the same kind of people. And I want that."

At the remote Porto Astro camp, a beautiful retreat on the majestic Aegean Sea, where refugees had to take a homemade barge to reach shore, Mahdi's transformation reached its culmination. Among Persian brothers in Christ, through hours of teaching, discussion, and fellowship, the stirring returned. The quiet photographer who had captured countless images of grace in exile became himself a portrait of divine transformation.

He accepted Christ and was baptized alongside five others—one Afghan among five Iranians—a living testament to how Christ dissolves the boundaries that divide humanity. The man who began as a translator for others' stories became himself a story of God's transforming power, his life now focused on a beauty no lens could capture but every heart could sense.

Questions for Reflection:

- How does God use our professional skills and circumstances to draw us to Himself?
- What role does observing authentic Christian community play in conversion?
- How do we recognize and respond to the "stirrings" of God in our lives?

Points for Prayer:

- For refugees seeking both physical and spiritual sanctuary
- For those serving in refugee ministries
- For the continued transformation of lives in refugee camps
- For more testimonies of reconciliation across ethnic divides
- For those experiencing the first stirrings of faith

Prayer Response:

Master Artist of souls, we marvel at how You paint stories of redemption on the canvas of displacement and doubt. Thank You for testimonies like Mahdi's that remind us how You work through quiet observation and consistent love to draw hearts to Yourself. Help us live authentically as Your people, knowing others are watching to see if our faith is real. May we, like Mahdi, learn to see beyond surface beauty to the transforming power of Your grace.

Grace in the Margins:

The Hooligans' Church in the Czech Republic

2020s

"It is not the healthy who need a doctor, but the sick...
I have not come to call the righteous, but sinners."

MATTHEW 9:12-13

I N THE MARGINS of Czech society, where addiction writes
its bitter stories and homelessness casts long shadows, God
was crafting a narrative of redemption that defied conventional
wisdom. Through the ministry of Marek Hust, the divine Author

was showing how His most powerful chapters often unfold in society's forgotten corners.

The story begins not in a pristine sanctuary but around breakfast and lunch tables, where the aroma of shared meals mingles with the fragrance of grace. But here, in these humble gatherings, those whom society labeled as "hooligans"—the addicted, the diseased, the troubled—found themselves drawn into a different story than the one their circumstances had written for them.

"We call ourselves 'Hooligans Church,'" Marek shares, his voice carrying both the weight of reality and the lift of hope. "It is our dream and vision that people from the streets would have a church to belong to." In this simple declaration lies a profound echo of Jesus's own ministry—how He consistently sought those whom religious society deemed untouchable, unworthy, beyond redemption.

The transformation extends beyond the streets into the stark confines of prison detention centers. Here, God's redemptive pen writes perhaps its most dramatic passages. One former criminal, whose vocabulary once consisted mainly of curse words and whose heart harbored only hatred for Marek, now sends greetings and requests prayer. The same man who once spewed venom now meets twice weekly to read Scripture and pray, his story a testament to how divine love penetrates the hardest shells of human resistance.

Through the distribution of Bibles in these unlikely spaces, eternal truth finds soil in hearts long hardened by life's cruelties. Each Scripture shared becomes more than mere words on a page – it becomes a seed of hope planted in ground that society had declared barren. The growth may be slow, but it is undeniably real, proving that God's Word truly does not return void.

Questions for Reflection:

- Where do we see "hooligans" in our own communities whom God might be calling us to reach?

- How does labeling people limit our vision of God's redemptive possibilities?
- What prejudices might we need to overcome to serve those society rejects?

Points for Prayer:

- For continued growth of the Hooligans Church
- For more workers willing to serve in challenging ministry spaces
- For transformation of lives affected by addiction and homelessness
- For hearts to be softened in prison ministry
- For wisdom in combining practical help with spiritual truth

Prayer Response:

Lord of the marginalized, we thank You for showing us through the Hooligans Church how Your love reaches into society's shadows. Thank You for servants like Marek who see beyond labels to the precious souls You died to save. Give us Your eyes to see potential where others see only problems, Your heart to love those whom society rejects. Help us create spaces of belonging for those who feel they don't belong anywhere. May we, like Jesus, be known as friends of sinners, carriers of hope to hopeless places.

Hope Behind Bars:

The Women's Prison Ministry

━━━

2020s

━━━

*"The Spirit of the Lord is on me, because he has
anointed me to proclaim good news to the poor."*

LUKE 4:18

I N THE STARK confines of Eastern European women's prisons, where gray walls and iron bars typically define the limits of
possibility, God was quietly orchestrating a revolution of hope.
Through the faithful witness of local believers, these spaces of confinement were becoming unexpected sanctuaries of transformation.
The story begins not with dramatic declarations but with simple

presence—believers willing to cross thresholds that most avoid, carrying God's Word into spaces where hope often struggles to survive. Each visit became a sacred appointment, each shared Scripture a seed planted in soil that society had deemed barren.

Among these concrete corridors and metal doors, something extraordinary began to take root. Women who had known only judgment found themselves encountered by grace. Those whom society had written off as irredeemable discovered their worth in divine eyes. Small groups began forming around shared Bibles, their pages worn by hands hungry for truth that transcends circumstance.

One particular inmate's transformation captured the essence of this quiet revival. Having received her first Bible, she spent countless hours absorbing its words, then began gathering others during free periods. What started as one woman's encounter with Scripture blossomed into regular Bible studies, proving that even prison walls cannot contain God's Word when it finds fertile heart-soil.

The guards noticed the change first—how women known for anger now exhibited unexpected peace, how those prone to despair began radiating hope. Some of these officers, intrigued by the transformation they witnessed, began asking questions about its source. The very authority figures tasked with confinement found themselves drawn to the freedom they saw in their charges' eyes.

Perhaps most remarkably, these prison Bible studies began redefining the meaning of family. Women separated from their children and loved ones discovered a different kind of belonging in their shared pursuit of truth. Letters home began carrying not just reports of hardship but testimonies of transformation, extending the impact of these prison revivals far beyond concrete walls.

Questions for Reflection:

- How does God's Word bring freedom even in physical confinement?

- Where do we see divine purpose in unlikely spaces?
- What "prisons" in our own lives need God's transforming truth?

Points for Prayer:
- For continued open doors in women's prisons
- For protection and wisdom for those leading prison ministry
- For transformed inmates to impact their families
- For more workers willing to serve in challenging spaces
- For the Word of God to bring hope in places of confinement

Prayer Response:
Lord of all freedom, we stand amazed at Your ability to transform places of confinement into spaces of spiritual liberation. Thank You for faithful servants who carry Your Word behind prison walls, for inmates whose transformed lives testify to Your power, and for the ripple effects that touch families and communities. Help us recognize that no space is too confined for Your Spirit to work. May we, like these faithful ministers, be willing to cross thresholds others avoid, carrying Your hope into every dark corner.

Vladimir's Ministry:

Love Beyond Grief

2020s

"He heals the brokenhearted and binds up their wounds."

PSALM 147:3

I N THE STREETS of Ukhta and Sosnogorsk, Russia, where July's gentle warmth softened the typically harsh landscape, a widower's grief was being transformed into an extraordinary testimony of grace. Vladimir's story reminds us how God often works His deepest ministry through our deepest wounds, turning personal loss into public witness.

July 22nd marked what would have been his wife Musa's birthday.

Instead of retreating into the quiet shadows of mourning, Vladimir chose to honor her memory in a way that captured her heart's greatest passion—sharing God's Word. With a folding table, a simple sign reading "Bible Free" on all four sides of his car, and a heart full of his wife's legacy, he embarked on a twenty-four-hour vigil of prayer and Bible distribution.

What began as a memorial gesture soon revealed a profound truth about authentic ministry. When a curious passerby asked the inevitable questions—"Who are you? Why are you distributing?"—Vladimir found himself sharing not just Scripture quotes but his personal story. The words flowed naturally: about his wife's passing two and a half years prior, about her love for the Bible, about this being her birthday gift to heaven.

In this vulnerability, Vladimir discovered something revolutionary: "This sincerity, this humanity breaks the ice of anti-sectarian sentiments and prejudices better and faster." Where formal evangelism might have met resistance, his genuine grief and love opened hearts. People began to see in him not a religious figure but a fellow human being touched by both loss and hope.

The impact was immediate and profound. Business cards were exchanged, relationships formed, and seeds planted that Vladimir believes will one day bloom into church membership. His discovery speaks to a deeper truth about ministry—that our wounds, when offered to God, often become the very channels through which His grace flows most freely to others.

Through Vladimir's story, we witness how public evangelism, often considered outdated, finds new life when infused with personal testimony and authentic emotion. His experience teaches us that sometimes our most effective ministry flows not from our strengths but from our scars, not from our victories but from our valleys.

Questions for Reflection:
- How might God want to use our own stories of loss for His purposes?
- What role does personal vulnerability play in effective ministry?
- Where might we be called to turn our grief into service?

Points for Prayer:
- For those transforming personal loss into ministry
- For wisdom in sharing personal stories effectively
- For more authentic connections in evangelism
- For hearts to be opened through genuine testimony
- For the legacy of faithful believers to bear fruit

Prayer Response:
Lord of all comfort, we thank You for showing us through Vladimir's story how You can transform our deepest grief into channels of Your grace. Thank You for those who choose to honor their loved ones by continuing their Kingdom work. Help us find courage to share our own stories of loss and hope. May we, like Vladimir, discover how authenticity and vulnerability can break down walls that arguments never could. Use our wounds as windows through which others might glimpse Your healing love.

A Policeman's Prayer:

Faith Born in Crisis

2020s

"I sought the Lord, and he answered me;
he delivered me from all my fears."

PSALM 34:4

I N THE EARLY days of the COVID-19 pandemic, when fear cast long shadows across Slovenia and isolation threatened to fragment communities of faith, God was orchestrating an encounter that would transform opposition into opportunity. The story unfolds in Nove Mesto, near the Croatian border, where a church's decision to seek divine guidance through prayer would lead to an unexpected harvest.

As the world grappled with lockdowns, Estera's church chose a path of spiritual resistance—not against authorities, but against the paralysis of fear. They committed to a week of prayer and fasting, seeking God's wisdom for sharing the gospel in a world suddenly changed. Their hearts' cry was simple yet profound: "Lord, show us how to reach hearts in this new reality."

Divine providence often works through misunderstanding. When a neighbor, viewing their gathering through the lens of pandemic restrictions, called the police, it seemed like an interruption of their spiritual pursuit. Two officers arrived, expecting to find lawbreakers, but God had appointed this moment for a different purpose altogether.

Dennis and Milena Turk, the group's leaders, faced the officers with grace and transparency. As they explained their gathering's purpose and shared the gospel with these unexpected visitors, what began as an investigation transformed into a divine appointment. One officer, his heart surprisingly tender, accepted their offer of a Christian book—a simple act that would bear extraordinary fruit.

Later, that same officer called Dennis back, his voice carrying the weight of spiritual awakening. The man who had come to investigate a potential violation now wanted to give his life to Christ and study the Bible more deeply. In God's divine economy, a neighbor's complaint had become the catalyst for eternal transformation.

But God wasn't finished wrapping gifts in the package of apparent opposition. A local online news reporter, spotting the police cars and suspecting a burglary, arrived to investigate. Instead of uncovering a crime story, he found himself drawn into God's narrative of redemption. The resulting article, titled "From the Police to the Blessing," included a video of Dennis sharing the Gospel—broadcasting God's truth far beyond the walls of their meeting place.

Questions for Reflection:

- How might God be using current restrictions or opposition in our lives as opportunities for His Kingdom?
- What "interruptions" to our plans might actually be divine appointments?
- How can we maintain a perspective of opportunity rather than opposition in challenging times?

Points for Prayer:

- For believers to recognize divine appointments in apparent opposition
- For wisdom in navigating restrictions while maintaining faithful witness
- For more testimonies of transformation from unexpected encounters
- For those in authority to encounter Christ through their duties
- For creative ways to share faith in challenging times

Prayer Response:

Master of divine appointments, we stand in awe of how You weave eternal purposes through temporal challenges. Thank You for reminding us through this officer's story that no circumstance is beyond Your redemptive touch. Help us see opportunities where others see obstacles, divine appointments where others see interruptions. May we, like Dennis and Milena, maintain grace under pressure and readiness to share Your truth even in unexpected moments. Transform our own encounters with authority into opportunities for Your Kingdom.

Rama's Calling:

Transforming Roma Communities with Faith

2020s

*"How beautiful on the mountains are the feet of those
who bring good news, who proclaim peace, who
bring good tidings, who proclaim salvation."*

ISAIAH 52:7

I N SERBIA, WHERE centuries-old Orthodox churches dot
the landscape but only zero point two percent of the population
actively practices Protestant faith, God was quietly raising up

leaders from the most unexpected places. Among the Roma people—often marginalized, typically poor, and scattered across Europe like modern-day Samaritans—a movement of the Spirit was taking root through a man named Rama.

In a culture where Roma people are typically relegated to the least desirable jobs—hand-harvesting fields or cleaning toilets—Rama emerged as a beacon of transformative faith. His face perpetually illuminated by an irrepressible smile, this Spirit-filled leader carried himself with a peace that seemed to defy his circumstances. Yet beneath his humble demeanor lay a story of multiplication that would challenge anyone's expectations.

Despite the discriminatory culture surrounding his community, Rama had helped plant seven churches in southern Serbia, nurturing a growing congregation of about 1,000 members. In a society where Roma people often struggle to find acceptance in mainstream establishments, these churches became sanctuaries of belonging and spiritual growth.

The depth of cultural barriers he was crossing became evident during a simple meal. When ministry partners invited Rama to eat with them in a public restaurant, they were unknowingly breaking significant cultural taboos. By Serbian standards, such an invitation to a Roma person was almost unheard of. Yet there sat Rama, grateful for the children's Bibles provided in the Roma dialect, his joy transcending social boundaries.

When asked about the remarkable growth among his people, Rama's answer cut to the heart of effective ministry: "Unity, discipleship, and church planting—these are the three things our churches are focused on." In these simple words lay a profound strategy that had helped transform lives across southern Serbia.

His own son's story served as a testament to changing times—securing employment in a Serbian factory, breaking through barriers that had long kept Roma people from such opportunities. Yet

Rama's focus remained not on societal advancement but on spiritual transformation, his humble leadership helping bridge ancient divides through the power of God's Word.

Questions for Reflection:

- How do we view and treat those our society marginalizes?
- What can we learn from Rama's three-fold focus on unity, discipleship, and church planting?
- Where might God be working through unexpected leaders in our own communities?

Points for Prayer:

- For the Roma people across Europe
- For continued growth and protection of the seven churches
- For more leaders like Rama to emerge from marginalized communities
- For breaking down of societal barriers and discrimination
- For unity among believers across ethnic and cultural divides

Prayer Response:

Lord of the marginalized, we thank You for servants like Rama who demonstrate Your power to work through those society often overlooks. Thank You for showing us again how Your Kingdom advances not through human privilege but through humble, faithful hearts. Help us see beyond cultural barriers to recognize Your image in every person. Give us wisdom to support and encourage those You are raising up as leaders from unexpected places.

Simple Acts, Profound Impact:

Ministry in Romanian Villages

2023

*"Let us not love with words or speech
but with actions and in truth."*

1 JOHN 3:18

I N THE QUIET corners of Romanian villages, where poverty often masks deeper spiritual hunger, God writes His stories not through grand gestures but through simple acts of compassion. Through the faithful ministry of Istvan and Adolf, we witness how divine love flows through channels of ordinary kindness, transforming mundane moments into sacred encounters.

Their ministry unfolds in the intimate spaces of daily life—on front porches where food baskets become vessels of hope, in quiet conversations where physical bread opens doors for the Bread of Life. Each encounter carries the weight of eternal possibility, each gesture of kindness a seed planted in soil prepared by hardship.

In the fabric of their ministry, we see threads of divine wisdom woven through human compassion. They understand that in a nation wrestling with economic challenges, physical needs often become bridges to spiritual conversations. Yet their approach carries a deeper insight—that true ministry must address both temporal and eternal hungers simultaneously.

Adolf, serving as EEM's representative in Romania, and Istvan, working in local outreach, have discovered something profound about God's economy of grace. In their experience, every act of physical provision becomes a potential moment of spiritual breakthrough. They've learned to watch for God's hand in the ordinary, to recognize divine appointments in daily encounters.

Their work stands as a testament to how God often chooses to reveal Himself not through dramatic interventions but through faithful presence. In a culture where trust must be earned and faith often is tested by immediate survival needs, their consistent care speaks volumes about the character of the God they serve.

Through their ministry, we glimpse how the Kingdom advances not primarily through programs or projects, but through personal encounters marked by genuine love. Each food basket delivered, each Bible shared, each conversation held becomes part of a larger tapestry of transformation that God is weaving across Romania.

Questions for Reflection:

- How might God be calling us to use ordinary moments for eternal purposes?
- Where do we see opportunities to meet both physical and spiritual needs?
- What role does consistent presence play in effective ministry?

Points for Prayer:

- For wisdom in balancing physical and spiritual ministry
- For more workers willing to serve in Romania's villages
- For divine appointments in daily encounters
- For resources to meet growing needs
- For hearts to remain sensitive to both visible and invisible hungers

Prayer Response:

Master of sacred moments, we thank You for servants like Istvan and Adolf who recognize Your hand in life's ordinary rhythms. Thank You for showing us how simple acts of kindness can become channels of eternal grace. Help us see the divine potential in every encounter, the sacred possibility in every interaction. May we, like these faithful workers, learn to minister to both body and soul with wisdom and compassion. Transform our ordinary moments into opportunities for Your extraordinary work.

Serhiyko's Light:

A Child's Faith in the Face of War

▬

2022

▬

"Let the little children come to me, and do not hinder them."

MATTHEW 19:14

I N THE WAR-TORN landscape of Kharkiv, Ukraine, where
artillery fire had become as common as birdsong, God was
weaving a story of redemption through the pure faith of a child.
Serhiyko, evacuated with his grandmother from besieged Kupyansk,
carried wounds deeper than physical scars—his mother had been
killed in recent shelling, leaving him to grapple with questions that
would challenge even the wisest adults.

Yet in the sterile corridors of a hospital where he and his grand-mother found refuge, something remarkable began to unfold. When asked for something to read, Serhiyko received a Children's Bible and an activity book. Instead of retreating into grief, this young soul's first response was to ask how to pray—not for himself, but for another boy in the hospital facing surgery.

In those quiet moments between the chaos of war, heaven touched earth through a child's simple faith. The same boy who had every reason to turn away from God instead turned to Him, asking profound questions about heaven—the new home of his beloved mother. But God wasn't finished with this story of multiplication through suffering.

Days later, his grandmother reached out again, not just for more Bibles and activity books, but because something extraordinary was happening. Serhiyko had found other children in the hospital—fellow orphans of war—and gathered them together to look at his Bible and color its pages. In the midst of their shared trauma, a children's Bible study was born, led by one who had endured the deepest loss.

The hospital ward, once echoing with the sounds of suffering, now resonated with the whispers of children discovering hope in ancient promises. His grandmother, watching this transformation, sought guidance herself—asking for materials to help her speak to these children about a God who remains present in life's darkest valleys.

What started as one child's encounter with Scripture had multiplied into a ministry of comfort and hope. In a place where death and loss cast long shadows, the light of God's Word shone through the pure faith of a child, reminding us that even in war's darkness, God's truth cannot be dimmed.

Questions for Reflection:

- How does childlike faith challenge our adult responses to tragedy?

- Where might God be using our own suffering to comfort others?
- What can we learn from Serhiyko's immediate impulse to pray for others?

Points for Prayer:

- For children traumatized by war in Ukraine
- For grandparents and guardians raising war-affected children
- For hospital ministries bringing God's Word to the suffering
- For the multiplication of faith through unlikely evangelists
- For healing and hope in war-torn regions

Prayer Response:

Father of the fatherless, we marvel at Your ability to bring light from darkness through the faith of a child. Thank You for Serhiyko's testimony that reminds us no circumstance is beyond Your redemptive touch. Comfort those who mourn, strengthen those who care for traumatized children, and multiply the impact of Your Word in places of suffering. Help us approach You with childlike faith even in life's darkest moments.

Intergenerational

Faith

—

Branko's Legacy:

Five Generations of Resilient Faith

2020s

"The Lord's love is with those who fear him, and his
righteousness with their children's children."

PSALM 103:17

I N A VILLAGE that has witnessed the rise and fall of nations, where each generation's birth certificate bears the name of a different country, Branko carries the torch of faith through storms of perpetual change. His story speaks not just of personal conviction, but of God's faithfulness across five generations of upheaval in a land where peace has been more poem than reality.

The weight of history rests heavily on Bosnia's soil. In Branko's village alone, four successive generations were born into different nations, each rebirth of the country bringing fresh wounds and ancient grievances. Yet in this crucible of constant change, Branko emerged as a mature Christian leader, his ministry stretching across a landscape where only shadows of faith remain.

In a nation where Christian materials are scarce—"The USA has far more options, such a luxury," he notes with gentle resignation—Branko finds himself stretched thin by the very abundance of spiritual hunger. Muslims approach him seeking Bibles for their children. Flood victims, stripped of material security, reach out for spiritual anchor points. Each request becomes a divine appointment, each Bible distributed a seed planted in soil watered by tears of desperation.

The paradox of war's impact on faith doesn't escape his notice. "War has opened hearts to God's Word," he observes, his voice carrying the weight of experience. "How precious it is when people ask for Bibles and not aid in the midst of war." In these words lies a profound truth about how human crisis often becomes divine opportunity, how the stripping away of earthly security can reveal eternal hunger.

When asked how to pray for Bosnia, his answer cuts through centuries of complexity with laser precision: "Real, genuine, spiritual revival." These words, spoken from a heart that has witnessed both the devastation of war and the persistence of hope, carry the authority of one who has learned to see God's hand even in history's darkest chapters.

Branko's ministry stands as a testament to faith that transcends national boundaries and survives political upheaval. In a region where instability has been the only constant for over five generations, his steady commitment to distributing God's Word provides an anchor of eternal truth in shifting sands of temporal change.

Questions for Reflection:

- How does God use societal upheaval to open hearts to His Word?
- What can we learn from believers who maintain faith through generational turmoil?
- How might our own periods of instability become opportunities for ministry?

Points for Prayer:

- For genuine spiritual revival in Bosnia
- For wisdom in distributing Bibles across religious boundaries
- For strength for leaders serving in resource-scarce environments
- For healing of generational trauma from repeated conflicts
- For continued openness to God's Word in times of crisis

Prayer Response:

Sovereign Lord of all generations, we thank You for faithful servants like Branko who demonstrate Your unchanging truth in ever-changing circumstances. Thank You for using even the upheavals of war to create hunger for Your Word. Grant us similar steadfastness in our own times of change, wisdom to recognize divine opportunities in human crises, and courage to maintain faithful witness through whatever storms may come. May we, like Branko, learn to see Your handwriting stories of redemption even in history's darkest chapters.

Lev's Testament:

A Child's Faith in Exile

2022

'And a little child shall lead them.'

ISAIAH 11:6

IN THE TENDER heart of a seven-year-old Ukrainian refugee named Lev, God began writing a story that would challenge our understanding of how faith flourishes in displacement. While adults grappled with the complexities of war and exile, this young soul discovered something profound in the pages of his first Bible—a foundation of stability that no conflict could destroy.

Croatia became Lev's place of refuge, far from the familiar streets and sounds of his Ukrainian hometown. Yet in this foreign land, where every word sounded strange and every face unfamiliar, God was preparing soil for seeds of faith to take root. When Lev received his Children's Bible from EEM, it became more than just a book—it transformed into a bridge between two worlds, a reminder that God's love knows no borders.

The beauty of God's work in Lev's life emerged in unexpected ways. As he learned to write for the first time, he chose to copy passages from his EEM-supplied Ukrainian Children's Bible, each carefully formed letter becoming both a language lesson and an act of worship. In these moments, what could have been mere academic exercise became sacred practice—a young refugee finding his voice through ancient words of truth.

But God wasn't finished. Lev's enthusiasm for Scripture proved contagious. Soon, this child who had lost so much began helping with local Bible distribution, his small hands passing out hope to others displaced by war. His presence at church became a testimony—not of loss, but of finding something greater than what had been left behind.

In Lev's story, we witness how God uses the youngest among us to remind us of essential truths: that faith can flourish in foreign soil, that ministry can flow from the hands of children, and that sometimes the purest expressions of trust come from those who have lost everything but found Christ.

Questions for Reflection:

- How might God be using the displaced people in your community as instruments of His grace?
- What can we learn from children about pure faith in times of crisis?
- Where do you see God turning losses into opportunities for ministry?

Points for Prayer:

- For refugee children adapting to new lands and languages
- For families separated by war to find hope in God's Word
- For churches welcoming displaced people
- For more children like Lev to become ministers of hope
- For the protection and spiritual growth of young believers in crisis

Prayer Response:

Father of the fatherless and Defender of widows, we thank You for young voices like Lev's that remind us of Your faithful love. In a world where displacement and loss threaten to overwhelm, You raise up children to show us the way to Your heart. Help us receive Your Kingdom as little children, finding in Your Word a home that cannot be shaken by war or circumstance. May we, like Lev, become instruments of Your hope wherever You plant us.

Revival in Samokov:

When God Breaks Down Walls

2023

*'Here there is no Gentile or Jew, circumcised
or uncircumcised, barbarian, Scythian, slave
or free, but Christ is all, and is in all.'*

COLOSSIANS 3:11

IN THE SHADOW of Bulgaria's Rila Mountains, where ancient prejudices have long drawn lines between Romani and Bulgarian communities, God is writing a story of reconciliation that defies generations of division. The testament of His work unfolds not in grand declarations, but in the simple, profound reality of children playing together, families worshiping as one, and love transcending the boundaries of ethnicity.

Samokov, a town of 35,000 souls, has become holy ground where God's redemptive work manifests in ways that challenge human understanding. Here, in what has become one of Bulgaria's largest church, something remarkable stirs—a movement where Romani and Bulgarian believers worship shoulder to shoulder, their voices rising as one in praise to the God who sees no distinction between His children.

The numbers tell part of the story—247 baptisms in a single day, over 1,000 gathered for Sunday worship, three services weekly filled with both Romani and Bulgarian faces. But the true miracle lies in the details: drug dealers finding redemption, poverty-stricken families discovering dignity, and children from both communities sharing desks in school—a sight once unimaginable in this region.

One church leader, his voice thick with emotion, shared the profound simplicity of their impact: "There are good rumors about us in the whole city." In a place where Romani people have historically been marginalized, these "good rumors" represent nothing less than a divine repositioning of human hearts.

The church's ministry extends beyond worship services into the very fabric of daily life. Every Monday through Friday, they serve meals to more than 70 orphans and widows. They provide shelter to the homeless, minister to the addicted, and build bridges between communities that have stood apart for generations. Each act of service becomes a brushstroke in God's masterpiece of reconciliation.

The youth of the church embody this transformation most vividly. Their worship team, composed of teenagers from both communities, leads services with a unity that speaks louder than any sermon. Their harmony becomes a prophetic declaration of God's Kingdom, where earthly divisions dissolve in the presence of divine love.

Questions for Reflection:
- What walls of division in your community is God calling you to help break down?
- How might your worship become a testimony of reconciliation?
- Where do you see God's "good rumors" spreading in unlikely places?

Points for Prayer:
- For continued unity between Romani and Bulgarian believers
- For the youth leading worship and bridging divides
- For multiplication of reconciliation ministries
- For wisdom in serving the marginalized
- For protection over this work of unity

Prayer Response:
Father of all nations, we stand in awe of Your power to unite what humanity has divided. Thank You for the testimony of Samokov, where Your love breaks down walls of prejudice and builds bridges of hope. Give us courage to cross the boundaries that separate us from our brothers and sisters. May our worship, like theirs, become a testimony to Your unifying love. Let Your "good rumors" spread through our communities until all Your children find their place at Your table.

Conclusion

A S WE CLOSE these pages, we stand in awe of how God writes His story through the most unexpected chapters of human history. From Gwen Hensley's first steps onto Vienna soil in 1961 to today's frontiers of faith, we witness a tapestry of divine faithfulness woven through decades of both triumph and tribulation.

These stories - each one a testament to how God's Word refuses to be bound—remind us that His truth flows like living water, finding its way through every crack in the walls of opposition. We've walked alongside Cardinals who became smugglers, witnessed Communist officials transform into evangelists, and seen children lead villages to faith. Each narrative whispers the same truth: when God's Word moves, nothing can stand in its way.

The landscape has changed dramatically since those early days of hidden Bibles and midnight border crossings. Where once believers risked everything to transport single copies of Scripture, now digital platforms carry God's truth across continents. Yet the heart of the mission remains unchanged - we want everyone to get it. Not just the physical pages, but the living truth that transforms lives and reshapes destinies.

In Ukrainian bomb shelters where elderly believers pore over large-print Bibles, in Romanian villages where children choose Scripture over chocolate, in Greek refugee camps where former enemies become brothers in Christ—we see the same hunger for truth that moved those first pioneers. God's Word continues to prove itself "alive and active," penetrating the darkest corners of human experience with divine light.

As we look toward tomorrow's horizons, we carry forward not just a ministry but a miracle - the miracle of how God uses ordinary people to accomplish extraordinary purposes. Whether through traditional pages or digital screens, in peaceful nations or war-torn regions, His Word continues to find those who hunger for truth.

To you who have journeyed through these stories with us—perhaps you've laughed, wept, or marveled at God's mysterious ways— we extend an invitation. The story isn't finished. God continues to write new chapters through willing hearts and open hands. Where might He be calling you to become part of this unfolding narrative?

Remember that small beginnings often yield the greatest harvests. A single Bible thrown from a train window multiplied into thirty believers. One child's faith sparked revival in a refugee camp. A moment of courage from an unlikely ally opened floodgates of truth across nations. What might God do through your simple act of obedience?

The needs remain vast—millions still wait for their first encounter with Scripture in their heart language. Yet we move forward with unshakeable confidence, knowing that the same God who parted seas for His people still makes paths where there seem to be none. His Word, like seed scattered on good soil, continues to yield harvests beyond human explanation.

As you close this book, may you carry with you, not just stories of what God has done, but vision for what He continues to do. May you be inspired to dream impossible dreams, to pray bold prayers, and to trust that the God who has proven faithful through generations remains faithful still. For wherever His Word goes forth, it never returns void.

The light still shines in the darkness, and the darkness has not, cannot, and will not overcome it.

"For as the rain and the snow come down from heaven and do not return there but water the earth, making it bring forth and sprout, giving seed to the sower and bread to the eater, so shall my word be that goes out from my mouth; it shall not return to me empty, but it shall accomplish that which I purpose, and shall succeed in the thing for which I sent it."

ISAIAH 55:10-11

TO LEARN MORE

The Bible. We Want Everyone To Get It.®
eem.org

NOTES

NOTES

NOTES

NOTES

NOTES

NOTES

NOTES